THE FUCHSIA BOOK

THE FUCHSIA BOOK

Borders • Bedding • Containers • Houseplants • Exhibiting

Allan Waddington

and

Philip Swindells

DAVID & CHARLES
Newton Abbot • London

[Frontis]
Bow Bells displays the typical
'Chinese lantern' flower form
of the fuchsia. Rather lax in
growth, this cultivar will need
support if grown as a bush
and is shown off to best
advantage in a hanging
pot or basket

British Library Cataloguing in Publication Data
Waddington, Allan
  The fuchsia book
  1. Fuchsias. Cultivation
  I. Title. II. Swindells, Philip
  635.9'3344

ISBN 0–7153–9076–7

Line illustrations by Jane Pickering
Typeset and designed by John Youé using a Macintosh system
and printed in Hong Kong by Wing King Tong Co Ltd
for David & Charles plc Brunel House Newton Abbot Devon

Distributed in the United States by Sterling Publishing Co Inc
387 Park Avenue South New York NY 10016-8810

Contents

1
Introducing
the Fuchsia

The cultivation of fuchsias is one of the fastest-growing gardening pursuits: not just their cultivation for decoration, but for exhibition as well. Even the species are now much sought after – although most are not highly decorative they have a quiet charm of their own which is attracting an increasing following. Of course, it is the wealth of hybrids and sports that have developed from these species (see Chapters 9 and 10) that most gardeners grow. Apart from green and bright, yellow, almost every colour imaginable can be found in their blooms, often several colours combining together to startling effect. Plant breeders are busy all the time improving flower quality and size, altering growth habits and developing hardiness. The fuchsia is a rapidly developing plant with a great future in the modern garden.

A lovely courtgard display of fuchsias and other bright flowers in containers, cleverly arranged on different levels so that all are shown off to best advantage

---

DR LEONHART FUCHS

The *Fuchsia* commemorates Dr Leonhart Fuchs who held the chair of medicine at the University of Tubingen from 1535 until 1566, although fuchsias were unknown to Europeans during the lifetime of Fuchs. It was not until 1703 that P. Carole Plumier recorded the generic name in his *Nova Plantarum Americanum* – a report of his plant-hunting expedition to the Americas. It is worth noting that today one of the finest collections of fuchsia species in Europe is maintained by that University in its botanical garden, and it is from there that many of the species in the extensive collection to be found at the gardens of the Northern Horticultural Society at Harlow Car originated.

This future is founded upon its versatility, for there are varieties that are suitable for every conceivable situation: short ones for bedding, tiny varieties for the rock garden or window box, hardy ones, tender ones, and those suitable for hedging, for mixing in the herbaceous border or growing as a tree-like standard to provide height in a bedding scheme. The wall of a lean-to greenhouse can be covered in climber-like fuchsias, and other varieties with the same lax habit (pendant growth) adapt equally well to a hanging pot or basket. Fuchsias respond to training (see Chapter 5) and can be turned into balls, pyramids, espaliers or fans. What other popular garden plant has such adaptability?

DISTRIBUTION OF FUCHSIA SPECIES

The origins of fuchsias are believed to lie in the Peruvian Andes. It is thought that from there they spread northwards to Mexico and Venezuela, and southwards to Tierra del Fuego. Apart from isolated populations in Brazil they did not progress far to the east, but westwards they spread across the Pacific to the far distant outposts of Tahiti and New Zealand. Although occurring in the tropics, no species can be regarded as truly tropical. Most grow at high altitudes, and although not frost hardy, are amenable to cool temperatures and humid conditions.

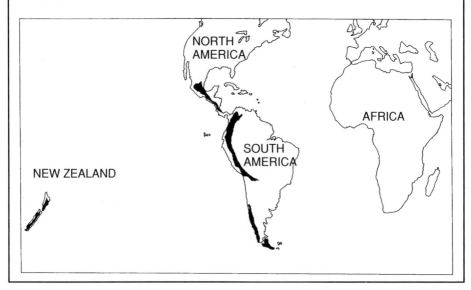

2
Garden Fuchsias

What better sight than a fuchsia trained around the porch of a house doorway? To obtain this form of growth against a wall regular pegging and tying in must be carried out, so that the plant or plants will grow upright. The greatest prerequisite, of course, is to live in the mildest parts of the country where there is very little risk of frost damage. But what a change from ivies or climbing roses

Fuchsias are most successful garden plants, but there are many misconceptions about their lack of hardiness. This is regrettable, for most of the varieties which are popularly grown indoors could equally well be established in the open. In fact, fuchsias are not hothouse subjects at all – they respond better to the cool, moist conditions that are fairly typical of our summer weather, especially in the north of England. Of course, the winter can cause problems for even the hardiest varieties if they are not well established. It therefore behoves the gardener to get his plants into the ground as soon as all danger of frost has passed, in order to obtain as long a growing season as possible.

HARDY FUCHSIAS

It is preferable to start in early summer with substantial plants, growing in minimum 10cm(4in) pots. Here in the north we dare not plant them out until the end of the first week in June with any confidence, but in other parts of the country it should be possible to plant towards the end of May. As the plants are likely to have been established from cuttings taken during the previous summer they will have spent all their life under glass, and while strong early growth is to be recommended it is important that they are properly hardened off. Before planting they should be exposed to life in a cold frame for two or three weeks – neglect in this respect will result in a certain amount of defoliation

9

and dieback after planting.

Good soil preparation is vital, the soil having been dug over the previous autumn and ample supplies of well-rotted animal manure or garden compost incorporated. A moisture-retentive soil is vital if fuchsias are to prosper, although care must be taken to ensure that manuring is not so heavy that soft growth is promoted. As with most decorative shrubs, hardy fuchsias can be expected to have a long and fruitful life, so it is essential that soil conditions are correct right from the start.

Well-weathered soil that was turned over the previous autumn should not be knocked down into a crumbly tilth until just before planting. If the soil is heavy and attempts are made to prepare it in advance there is the risk of heavy rain compacting the soil surface and making planting conditions unpleasant and difficult. Not that loose, puffy soil is any more desirable: before planting a bed, shuffle across the surface of the soil slowly with both feet. This will firm it gently without compaction and provide ideal conditions for getting the plants in.

Planting

When planting, ensure that the rootball of each plant is thoroughly soaked. Fuchsias that have been grown in soil-less compost will have difficulty in breaking out if the compost is not really damp at planting time. The plants should be firmed in, planting slightly deeper than their previous soil line.

Make a hole about 7cm(3in) deeper than the pot depth. For example, if the plant is in a 12.5cm(5in) pot, then the hole should be 20cm(8in) deep. Sprinkle some peat and a little bonemeal around the inside of the hole, and mix the bottom up a little. After knocking the plant out of the pot, just tease open the roots by putting slight pressure on the compost and squeezing gently. Place the plant at the bottom of the hole and then backfill until level with the compost of the plant, leaving around 7cm(3in) still to fill in. This should be carried out over the next two months by occasionally scraping

When planting a hardy fuchsia in the garden first prepare the hole, then add some peat and a sprinkling of bonemeal. Ensure that the hole is deep enough for the rootball of the fuchsia to be 7cm (3in) below ground level when planting is complete, in order to avoid frost damage. Firm in well

some of the backfill soil into the hole and between the branches. Once this depression has been filled in, planting is complete. Apart from making watering easier and more effective, this routine allows for the gradual buildup of compost, which should be scattered regularly amongst the branches during the summer months. This provides stability for new plants and, in the presence of soil moisture, dormant buds on the buried stem are encouraged to sprout new shoots and create much bushier plants. This deeper planting also helps to protect the rootstock during severe winter weather.

Cultivation
Summer cultivation of hardy fuchsias largely consists of watching out for whitefly, greenfly and similar pests and ensuring that the plants do not dry out, especially in the early stages of their establishment. Each spring, it is useful to mulch around the plants with a generous layer of shredded bark or well-rotted garden compost

Tom Thumb is seen at its best when growing naturally outdoors like this. Also grown by many exhibitors as a single-flowered mini-standard

in order to conserve moisture. If newly established plants do not break readily and form a shapely bush, they should be encouraged to do so by regularly pinching out. Never be frightened to pinch back unruly shoots. It is strange, but true, that fuchsias which are grown outside usually produce a much better shape quite naturally than their indoor counterparts, which have the benefit of their pots being turned at regular intervals. Incidentally, flower colour outside is also noticeably more intense.

Ideally, faded blossoms should be removed from hardy kinds as regularly as from those grown as pot plants. Unfortunately this is not always a practical proposition where large plants or groups are involved. Otherwise, nothing need be done until the spring, the retention of all old wood for the winter months being essential for the survival of the plants. Although in the majority of hardy fuchsia trials, they are left to their own devices during the winter – primarily because we are assessing their hardiness – many gardeners provide added protection by covering the base of the plants with ashes or dried bracken, etc.

Cutting down the old stems of overwintered hardy fuchsias is best left until May. Many gardeners await the appearance of the first green shoots before taking the secateurs to the plants. This is fine if you can be ruthless, for the quite natural temptation is to leave shoots which emerge part way up a stem, whereas correct practice decrees that plants should be cut down to the ground to encourage the proliferation of basal shoots and ultimately bushier plants, especially in the north where all the wood will be dead anyway.

After pruning, give each plant a generous handful of bonemeal. This is a slow-release fertiliser which will sustain growth, but not induce winter-vulnerable succulence. Once proficiency and experience in the cultivation of hardy fuchsias has been gained, then the selective use of a foliar feed should be investigated. In the hands of the uninitiated it can promote both disease and winter-hardiness problems.

Root area mulched with ashes, peat, straw or leaves to give extra frost protection

Using Hardy Fuchsias

Hardy fuchsias can be used in many ways in the garden, but if intended as permanent inhabitants it should be realised that except in the mildest parts of the country their role will be restricted to providing splashes of colour in the border, although in favoured localities they can be used to great effect as a hedge.

In the Border

The possibilities for planting schemes are endless. A fuchsia used as a dot plant is just that — a plant which is positioned in the scheme so that it catches the eye immediately.

A large bush fuchsia or two would be ideal planted in a bed made up of annual or biennial plants such as petunias, geraniums, salvias, small dahlias, the grey-leaved cineraria, antirrhinums, calendula and many more. A good, large bush plant can also be planted into an already established shrubbery, where the colour will stand out superbly once it is in full bloom. A shrubbery of green-leaved, seldom-flowering shrubs with a few fuchsias dotted here and there will give a beautiful contrast, even more so when the fuchsias have become established over a few years and made quite sizeable plants. With the colours of the autumn leaves turning to reveal their full glory the fuchsia will still be in flower, and will stand out as perhaps the *only* shrub in flower in the border.

Standard fuchsias are better used in larger flowering schemes where quite a few plants can be incorporated.

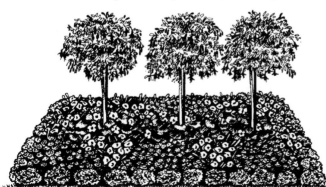

Here, standard fuchsias have been used as centrepieces for a general bedding scheme. Seen rising above the colourful geraniums, calendulas, petunias and many other bedding out plants, which are available in more colours than ever before, the fuchsia grown as a standard is outstanding

13

They can look good set in a row across the centre of a bed, underplanted again with annual and biennial flowering schemes. In fact, an ideal way to show a standard fuchsia at its best is to have only a small piece of ground cultivated, just large enough to hold one standard plant, with the outer circle or square edged with alternate plants of lobelia and alyssum. A garden pathway or walk which has a border at least two feet wide running alongside it is an ideal siting for a row of standard fuchsias, just as a row of standard roses might be planted (but without the thorns!).

Use the small-flowered, low-growing cultivars for edging a border, or perhaps as dot plants in a rockery. If the bed or border is to be planted up using only fuchsias, then it is a good idea to plant them in groups of a minimum of three of the same cultivar. This gives the patterned effect of a group, rather than a muddled hotchpotch of all different cultivars, which provides no contrast at all.

Hedging

It is important when selecting cultivars for a hedge that only tough, vigorous kinds are chosen. Even then, it must be accepted that in severe winters the hedge may be cut to the ground. So while we would wholeheartedly recommend fuchsias as colourful hedging subjects, their weaknesses cannot be neglected.

If a fuchsia hedge is contemplated, remember that a lot of groundwork needs doing first. A good hedge does not just happen, it originates from careful soil preparation, together with the judicious selection of cultivars. If the soil along the intended line of the hedge is very heavy and prone to waterlogging in the winter, then adequate drainage must be provided. A layer of rubble or a proper plastic or tile land-drain should be installed at least 60cm(2ft) below the surface, preferably leading to a soakaway. Wet patches or uneven soil quality is reflected in the stature of the hedge, often leading to unsightly gaps appearing. When preparing the soil remove all weeds, especially those of a peren-

HOWLETTS
HARDY

GRACILIS VARIEGATA

nial nature – bindweed and couch grass will rapidly swamp a newly planted hedge. Remember that this is the last opportunity in the life of the hedge to get at the soil, so ensure that it is adequately enriched with well-rotted organic matter and is well cultivated.

Planting follows along the same lines as those advocated for fuchsias used for border decoration (see p10). Depending on the cultivar being used, plant at between 45 and 75cm(1½ and 2½ft) intervals either in a single, straight line or in an alternate, triangular fashion. As it is hoped that a fuchsia hedge will become a permanent feature, the new plants should be encouraged to sprout from the base by regularly pinching back the shoots. This should ensure the development of a sturdy framework, for not only are fuchsia hedges vulnerable to winter frosts killing their stems, but the weight of snow on lank, rapidly-produced branches can be equally devastating.

Other Uses for Hardy Fuchsias

Apart from the uses described, hardy fuchsias can also be accommodated in patio planters and tubs in the same way as their more tender counterparts. However, they cannot become permanent inhabitants as they rarely overwinter successfully. Frost kills the roots during most winters, as the compost in which they are growing is exposed to the cold from all directions.

Planting a fuchsia hedge. As when planting any fuchsia in the garden, ensure that the crowns of the plants are well below soil level, and set them 45-75cm (1½-2ft) apart

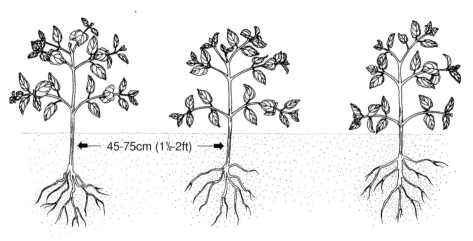

◄— 45-75cm (1½-2ft) —►

Fuchsias in tubs must be regarded as temporary inhabitants of the summer garden, and should be replaced with spring-flowering bedding plants each autumn.

Reliable Hardy Fuchsias

In the following list, fuchsias marked * are growing in the trial beds of the British Fuchsia Society at Harlow Car Gardens in Harrogate. These were originally planted in 1984. Most other cultivars listed can be seen either in the trial display of the Knaresborough and District Fuchsia Society (at Harlow Car Gardens) which goes back to the 1960s, or growing in mixed beds and borders throughout the gardens at Harlow Car.

The British Fuchsia Society produces a list of recommended hardy fuchsias, so if you are in any doubt about the potential hardiness of a cultivar not noted here we urge you to consult the Society.

See p25 for an explanation of the abbreviations used, and Appendix 2 for explanations of botanical terms. The date of introduction and name of breeder/introducer is given in brackets.

Fuchsia magellanica A variable hardy species from South America with many botanical varieties. It was this that was used by hybridisers in the early development of modern garden varieties. Rarely grown in its original form. (1768)

F.m. var. alba See *F.m. var. molinae.*

F.m. var. americana elegans Small flowered. Tube and sepals scarlet; corolla purple. (HC, 1929)

F.m. var. discolor Dwarf habit. Tube and sepals red; corolla mauve.

F.m. var. globosa Compact habit. Tube and sepals scarlet; corolla purple. Conspicuously globose buds.

FUCHSIAS FOR HEDGING

Raised in 1860, Madame Cornellissen has withstood the challenge of the many cultivars introduced since to remain a favourite for hedging. Perhaps the best cultivar to have come out of Belgium

The persistence of a fuchsia hedge is very much dependent upon the winter climate. All the popular kinds used for hedging are perfectly hardy, but in severe weather they may be cut to ground level. Those recommended here will all regenerate, but it may take twelve months or more for the hedge to become completely reinstated. While mulching of the soil around hardy fuchsias during the autumn in cold areas provides root protection, nothing practical can be done to protect the aerial parts of the plant from severe frosting and bark splitting. This is a hazard that must be lived with, and the reason why most gardeners regard fuchsia hedges as better internal divisions than boundary markers.

Fuchsia magellanica var. molinae   Madame Cornelissen
F. m. 'Riccartonii'   Margaret
Chillerton Beauty   Margaret Brown
Drame   Mrs Popple

F.m. var. globosa 'Dunrobin Bedder'. Neat dwarf habit. Tube and sepals red; corolla violet-purple. Small-flowered, but profuse. (1890, Melville)

F.m. var. gracilis Tube and sepals red; corolla purple. Slender blossoms borne beneath delicate arching branches. Vigorous. (HC, 1929)

F.m. var. gracilis variegata As *F.m. var. gracilis,* but with silvery variegated leaves. At Harlow Car it needs constant attention in order to prevent uncoloured foliage taking over. Any plain shoots should be removed immediately they are noticed. (HC, 1962)

F.m. var. longipedunculata A variety of the species with longer blossoms and lilac-mauve corollas.

*F.m. var. molinae (syn. F.m. var. alba) A very tough character that prospers at Harlow Car. Tube and sepals white with a pinkish cast. Sepals often distinctly flushed with lilac. Corolla fading to lilac-pink. Excellent for general garden use in the mixed border.

F.m. 'Riccartonii' The most widely grown and amongst the most reliable hardy cultivars of fuchsia. Allegedly a seedling from *F.m. var. globosa* in the Riccarton garden of Sir William Gibson near Edinburgh, it is regarded by others as a mere variant of *F. magellanica.* In many parts of the country it attains permanent shrubby proportions, often being used for hedging in the more equitable climates of Ireland and the Isle of Man. In such situations it may attain a height of 1.2-1.5m(4-5ft) – at Harlow Car it is regularly cut to the ground and behaves like an herbaceous plant. Tube and sepals bright red; corolla purple. Sometimes produces small black berries. (c1835) (AM, 1966) (FCC, 1978)

F.m. var. thompsonii A rarely encountered variety. Tube and sepals bright scarlet; corolla pale purple. (AM,1965)

19

Hardy Cultivars of Multiple and Indeterminate Parentage

*Abbe Farges Semi-double. Tube and sepals cerise, the latter markedly reflexed. Corolla lilac-rose. Flowers profusely but has very brittle wood which is easily broken. Not suitable for an exposed or windy garden. Upright bushy habit. (1901, Lemoine) (HC, 1965)

Achievement Single. Tube and sepals cerise-red, the latter recurved. Corolla reddish-purple with a scarlet base. Blossoms large and freely produced. Foliage pale green. Upright habit. One of the easiest hardy cultivars. (1886, Melville)

*Alice Hoffman Semi-double. Tube and sepals rose-pink; corolla white with rose-pink veins. Small flowers freely produced amongst bronze-green foliage. Bushy upright habit. One of the most reliable hardy fuchsias to be found anywhere. (1911, Klese)

Beacon Single. Tube and sepals deep pink; corolla bright mauvish-pink. Medium-sized blossoms. Free-flowering and of a neat, bushy, upright habit. (1871, Bull) (HC, 1978)

*Charming Single. Tube carmine, reflexed sepals reddish-cerise; corolla rosy-purple lightening to cerise at base. Foliage yellowish-green fading at tips of leaves. Medium-sized flowers and distinctive upright habit. (1895, Lye) (AM, 1929)

*Chillerton Beauty Single. Tube and sepals rose-pink tipped with green. Corolla mauve-violet with pink veining. A robust cultivar well suited to growing as a hedge. (1847, Bass) (HC, 1962; AM, 1978)

*Cliff's Hardy Single. Tube and sepals light crimson tipped with green; corolla violet-blue, paler towards the base and with scarlet veining. Blossoms medium sized and held erect. Upright habit. (1966, Gadsby) (AM, 1978)

*Corallina Single. Tube and sepals scarlet; corolla purple, pinkish at base. Very distinctive dark coppery-green foliage carried on spreading branches and forming a rather lax bush. A good vigorous cultivar that has prospered in the open at Harlow Car for many years. (1884, Pince) There is apparently a variegated foliage kind – 'Corallina Variegated' – which was introduced from the Institut Horticole, Liege, Belgium, in 1983, but this is not yet widely grown, nor do we have any experience with it yet at Harlow Car.

*Display Single. A self pink; tube and sepals rose-pink; corolla deep pink. Not considered as a reliably hardy fuchsia everywhere, although it overwinters in most parts of Britain if given a generous protective mulch of ashes or old bracken during the autumn. (1881, Smith) (HC, 1931)

Drame Semi-double. Tube and sepals scarlet; corolla violet-purple. Medium-sized blossoms freely produced amongst pale green foliage. Habit compact, but spreading. Useful for a low informal hedge. (1880, French)

*Eleanor Rawlins Single. Tube and sepals carmine-red; corolla magenta shading to carmine at base. Medium-sized blossoms produced freely amongst light green foliage. Although perfectly hardy it serves well as a summer bedding cultivar. (1954, Wood)

*Elfin Glade Single. Tube and sepals pink; corolla pinkish-mauve. Medium-sized blossoms on an upright bushy plant. (1963, Colville) (AM, 1963)

Empress of Prussia Single. Bright scarlet tube and sepals; corolla reddish-magenta. Easily recognised as it carries six to eight blossoms in each leaf joint instead of the more usual two. Upright bushy habit. (1868, Hoppe)

*Flash Single. Tube and sepals light magenta; corolla light red. Flowers small but borne in profusion. Upright bushy habit with light green foliage. (*c* 1930)

*Genii Single. Tube and sepals red, corolla violet shading to deep rose. Primarily grown for its bright golden foliage. The hardiest of the golden-leafed cultivars. Neat compact habit. Should be in every fuchsia collection. (1951, Reiter)

*Lady Thumb Semi-double. Tube and sepals pale reddish-carmine; corolla white lined with carmine. Free-flowering, dwarf habit. Very hardy and well suited to rock garden cultivation. (1966, Roe) (FCC, 1978)

Lena Semi-double. Tube and sepals flesh-pink; corolla magenta-rose. Medium-sized blossoms freely produced on a plant of lax habit. (1862, Bunney)

Madame Cornelissen Semi-double. Tube and sepals deep scarlet; corolla white with cerise veining. Small-flowered, prolific, attractive, dark green leaves. Strong upright habit, well suited to hedging. (1860) (AM, 1965)

Left:
A large hardy fuchsia makes an excellent combination with a white hydrangea and dark-leaved berberis in this well-planned garden

Right:
An excellent, tall, hardy fuchsia, we can thoroughly recommend Margaret as a tough plant with the ability to flower on and on

*Margaret Semi-double. Tube and sepals carmine-scarlet; corolla violet with cerise veining. Very vigorous with medium to large blossoms carried in profusion. An excellent hedging cultivar. (1939, Wood)

Margaret Brown Single. Tube and sepals rose-pink; corolla light rose. Small flowers in profusion amongst light green foliage. Will make a satisfactory hedge. (1949, Wood)

Mrs Popple Single. Tube and sepals scarlet; corolla purple-violet, cerise towards the centre. A vigorous hardy plant with spreading bushy foliage heavily laden with blossoms. A first class plant grown anywhere, even on a heavy clay soil structure. Makes a good low hedge. (1899, Elliott) (FCC, 1965)

Mrs W.P. Wood Single. Tube and sepals pale pink; corolla white. A profusion of small flowers amongst light green foliage. Upright and bushy. (1949, Wood)

*Nicola Jane Double. Tube and sepals rose-pink tipped with green. Corolla mauve with pink veining. A tall-growing cultivar which is excellent for hedging. (1959, Dawson)

*Papoose Semi-double. Tube and sepals red; corolla dark purple. Small-flowered but prolific. (1960, Reedstrom)

*Pixie Single. Tube and sepals pale cerise, corolla rose-mauve fading toward base and veined with carmine. Foliage pale yellowish-green with distinctive red veining. Neat, upright, bushy habit. Well suited as a hedge. (1960, Russell) (HC, 1978)

*Rose of Castile Single. Tube and sepals white tipped with green. Sepals sometimes show a pale pink flush. Corolla purple fading to white at the base, somewhat pinkish flushed. Small- to medium-sized flowers produced in abundance on an upright bushy plant. (1855, Banks)

*Rose of Castile Improved Single. Tube and sepals flesh-pink; corolla violet-purple. Blossoms medium-sized. Altogether more vigorous than the original cultivar. (1869, Banks) (HC, 1931)

*Rufus (*syn.* **Rufus the Red**) Single. Bright red self-coloured. Medium-sized flowers freely produced. Upright bushy habit. Excellent for bedding. (1952, Nelson) (AM, 1978)

Son of Thumb Single. Tube and sepals cerise; corolla lilac. Small blossoms, but very free flowering and compact. Ideal for the rock garden. A sport from 'Tom Thumb'. (1978, Gubler).

*Tom Thumb Single. Tube and sepals carmine; corolla mauve with carmine veination. Small-flowered but very prolific. Dwarf compact habit. Ideal for the rock garden. (1850, Baudinot) (FCC, 1962).

Trase Semi-double/double. Tube and sepals carmine-cerise; corolla flushed white and veined carmine-cerise. Free-flowering, medium-sized blossoms on an upright bushy plant. A good specimen plant for the border. (1959, Dawson) (AM, 1978)

HC	Highly Commended by the Royal Horticultural Society.
AM	Award of Merit of the Royal Horticultural Society following hardiness trials.
FCC	First Class Certificate of the Royal Horticultural Society following hardiness trials.

BEDDING FUCHSIAS

Growing fuchsias as bedding plants is not as popular as it ought to be. This is largely because purchased plants are expensive when compared with other seed-raised bedding. It is true that fuchsias are easily grown from cuttings, even if you have no more elaborate a propagating facility than the kitchen windowsill. However, rooting the cuttings is one thing, overwintering the young plants is quite another. Even if you have a greenhouse, the prospect of providing protection for sufficient plants to make a bedding display is quite daunting.

The best and most weatherproof fuchsias for bedding come from amongst the ranks of the hardy cultivars. It is these that perform the most consistently. However, they have to be treated in a totally different manner from when they are used as hardy border

A collection of fuchsias bedded out in Mr Heaton's Sutton-in-Craven garden. With the fuchsias set off against a beech hedge and bordered by begonias and pansies, a delightful flow of colour has been achieved

FUCHSIAS FOR BEDDING

The cultivars recommended here include the tough, reliable, hardy ones that make good bedding subjects as well as some of the most suitable tender varieties. When planting either the same rules apply, for each are as vulnerable as the other in the young plant stage to damage by frost. Even large plants should not be put out until the danger of frost has passed, and all must receive liberal quantities of water until well established. There is no such thing as permanent bedding.

An extremely floriferous red-and white cultivar, Lady Thumb is at its best when grown as a hardy in the garden border. Here it provides excellent contrast with the spiky form of the heathers which surround it

Hardy Cultivars
Alice Hoffman
Drame
Dunrobin Bedder
Eleanor Rawlins
Genii (for foliage effect)
Lady Thumb
Rufus
Son of Thumb
Tom Thumb

Tender Cultivars
Bunny
Cloth of Gold (for foliage effect)
D-Day 44
Ken Jennings
Margaret Roe
Perry Park
Strawberry Delight

plants. They should be propagated and grown on in the manner advocated for tender cultivars (see Chapter 4) and their duration in the garden should be just the same. The fact that they are hardy should be ignored. At the end of the season the plants must be discarded, or dug up and potted to overwinter indoors for use next year.

Purchasing Bedding Plants

Apart from standard fuchsias, which are used as 'dot' plants in bedding schemes and maintained from year to year, most other bedding fuchsias are purchased on an annual basis. The difficulty of overwintering young plants, or forcing old plants to produce early cuttings, makes the purchasing of plants a sensible proposition for the ordinary gardener. Such plants will have received a very general cultural regime, having been pinched out to ensure a good stocky habit, but beyond that will not have been given any specialist attention. Not that they need any, for fuchsias that are grown for bedding quickly become part of an overall picture and are not recognisable as individuals. Providing that purchased plants are of reasonably even growth and can fulfill their role they will be adequate.

However, it is important when purchasing plants to make sure that they are not under stress. This can be caused by a number of factors, but most usually is associated with being potbound and not receiving sufficient water. Ideally, buy plants that have just filled their pots with roots. If, on removing a plant from a pot, the rootball is malleable when gently squeezed, then the plant is likely to be in good order. If the rootball is solid with root, then the plant is potbound, likely to be under stress, and will not establish readily without the rootball being disrupted, which in turn will give the plant a check.

Obviously, purchased plants should be healthy, free from any signs of whitefly or fungal disease and clothed with foliage to the base. The latter is a clear indication that a plant has been cultivated without stress. Plants with naked bases should be avoided, as should those that have widely spaced leaf joints or sparsely branched stems. Remember that the bedding plant season is relatively short and that plants must get off to a good start if the longest possible period of colourful blossoms is to be enjoyed.

Cultivation
The preparation of the soil and the planting procedure follow along similar lines to those advocated for the hardy kinds (see above). However, it is vital in a formal bedding display that distances between plants are such that the foliage touches and completely hides the soil. Plant densities must therefore be carefully assessed and numbers not skimped. In order to anticipate the behaviour in your garden of a particular cultivar it is necessary to have some prior knowledge. A well-ordered bedding scheme can only be implemented successfully with the intimate knowledge and personal experience of the cultivars to be used. When the plants are to serve as focal points or 'dot' plants, then this depth of experience is not so important.

Unlike hardy fuchsias, standard and specimen plants that are accommodated in the garden for the summer months can merely be plunged into the soil in their pots to make lifting easier in the autumn. While this works well, it only does so if particular attention is paid to careful planting and aftercare. It is essential that the pot rims are well below soil level in order to provide the plants with a cool root run. This is vital when fuchsias are growing in clay pots, for, if the rim is exposed to the air, moisture is withdrawn and, in hot weather, warmth is transmitted.

As the plants are constrained by their pots, particular attention must be paid to watering and liquid feeding. Remember that the opportunities for root expansion are minimal and any that pass through the drainage holes of the pots are unlikely to make significant difference to the plants. In fact, water and feed pot-restricted fuchsias outdoors in much the same way

hedge and monitoring the behaviour of varieties being grown by your neighbour. Similarly, the exchange of local information at fuchsia society meetings will also prove useful.

FUCHSIAS IN OUTDOOR CONTAINERS

Choosing the Plants

Patio containers come in a wide range of sizes and shapes, but the role of the plants in each is the same: to provide a balanced mound of colourful fuchsia, which sweeps down and visually unites the container with its plants. The plants should not appear as if they have just been put into the top, except inevitably at the very

---

A WINDOWBOX DISPLAY

Windowboxes present greater problems than tubs and planters, for the amount of compost is often more limited and so root competition is greater. Short growing fuchsias suit the situation best: for compact and more upright growth choose Tom Thumb or Lady Thumb. If a pendant habit is required try Derby Imp, Harry Gray, the strong-growing pink, Jack Shahan, Red Marinka or white-and-purple La Campanella and, preferably, do not mix with other plants. However, when growing short upright kinds it is appropriate to mix them with scrambling plants which will hang down over the container, best of all being the trailing lobelias. The common trailing blue or Cascade types are ideal, for these have a neat habit and a non-competitive root system. They are also of a uniform colour. Other more colourful, but less scandent, mixed kinds like String of Pearls are available, but these are only suited to bright, rainbow-like design arrangements.

An alternative scheme could use the nearly self, reddish-pink Beacon Rosa, either on its own or in combination with its parent plant, the much deeper Beacon. The nearly self, pink culti-

var Display is another possibility. At the front of the box use in contrast white alyssum, and then for trailing over the front edge plant ivy with trailing geraniums of deeper red cultivars such as Doctor Chipault, Wyck Beacon or the lovely red-and-white Rouletta. Put in one or two plants of trailing white-and-green nepeta too. For a different effect, plant up with pink geraniums such as the Irene cultivar named Penny, or the lovely bright pink Springtime, while for maximum impact you could use the number one brilliant crimson bedding geranium Highfields Pride, or its scarlet seedling Duchess of Devonshire. Instead of geraniums, you could of course use either the multiflora flowering begonias or the lovely tuberous begonias in red, pink or yellow.

The possibilities for using fuchsias in windowbox displays, whether alone or in combination with other plants, are almost endless. The range of colour and habit is immense – even that special mini-standard is ideal to plant in a windowbox, which will be just the correct height to show it at its best.

---

beginning of their life. This demands the use of cultivars with varying habits, the plants around the perime-
ter of the container having a pendant habit, with those
towards the centre being progressively more upright,
and the tallest plant of all filling the centre. Foliage
colour and contrast should not be neglected, for there
are some excellent golden and variegated fuchsias
available.

Whatever you decide to use, remember that it is
better to grow just two or three cultivars in a container,
rather than have every plant different. With some of
the fuchsias that have a lax habit it is often possible to
plant the container entirely with a single kind and
obtain a quite striking effect. For hanging pots and
hanging baskets, more than anywhere else in the
garden, it is important to have a uniformity of growth
and habit, and this can only be achieved easily by the
use of a single cultivar.

Choosing a Container

Almost any container can be used to accommodate
fuchsias, providing that it has sufficient depth for
compost and suitable drainage arrangements. Garden
centres are full of a whole range of elegant and decorative planters in materials as diverse as plastic and

Below:
The cultivars Thalia and
Gold Runner are ideal
for a patio container in
sunshine. Here they
are seen to advantage in
a plastic urn, successfully
combined with
trailing ivy

Right:
A glorious column of flower:
fuchsias can be grown
in a wide range of different
containers, either on their
own or, as here, combined
with a variety of other
colourful plants

reconstituted stone. All can find a place in the garden. Indeed, it is up to the gardener to select something that is to his or her taste, but within this choice the wellbeing of the fuchsias and their appearance must be considered. Container design is therefore very important.

Any windowbox or planter must have a *minimum* depth of 15cm(6in) if it is to allow proper root development, and a greater depth is desirable. With this in mind, avoid any containers (especially urns) which are shallow round the outside, for if the outer planting is unable to penetrate into the centre of the container it will constantly dry out and the plants will be permanently under stress. Drainage must also be provided, preferably by holes in the base of the container or windowbox. In containers without holes, a generous layer of gravel in the bottom will often suffice if watering is very carefully attended to.

Planting the Container

Tubs, planters, windowboxes and hanging baskets are very attractive additions to the garden, but they need careful attention if they are always going to look their best. Success with any container is based upon the choice of fuchsia cultivars and the compost that it contains. The wrong medium and unsuitable varieties make it difficult for even the most skilful gardener to produce an attractive display.

Composts should be moisture retentive, yet free draining. In tubs, planters and windowboxes it is best to use John Innes Potting Compost No 2 with at least one third by volume of sedge peat added. Hanging baskets are a different proposition, for it is obviously helpful if they are light in weight. Soil-less composts within a sphagnum moss lining are best in this case, and as it is always difficult to maintain moisture in a hanging basket because of the constant drying effects of the wind, it is wise to add a little perlite. This is a white, granular material derived from a volcanic rock, which is capable of absorbing moisture and allowing it to be released back into the compost in drier periods. Up to a quarter by volume of perlite can be added to good effect.

Modern hanging pots are made of plastic and not given to rapid desiccation. Culturally excellent, they are, however, mostly aesthetically poor and do not compare with the traditional wire basket with its lining of green sphagnum moss. These baskets are not as difficult to establish as one might imagine: the moss layer is built up gradually as the compost is added. Nowadays, sphagnum moss is in short supply and is expensive when you are able to get it. Ready made linings are available at most garden centres, and are made of peat, foam etc. One of the most popular ways to line a basket is by using a plastic bag, and black is by far the best colour to use – nothing looks worse than a lining of multicoloured plastic with wording and pictures on it. Whatever you use, make quite sure that slits are made in the plastic to enable surplus water to drain away, and so prevent any danger of waterlogging.

Watering

If a watering can is used on a newly planted basket the water will often flow irregularly through the open sides. It is always better to soak these in a deep bowl until the compost has settled, taking care to avoid damaging any trailing shoots. A watering can may be used subsequently, providing that it is fitted with a fine

---

SITING A WINDOWBOX

The choice of styles for planting up windowboxes is almost infinite. Before you begin, however, remember that the plants do have to be fed and watered frequently – so think carefully before placing the box in its final position. For example, a large number of windowboxes are placed on brackets of shelving below the windowsill and, if the window is of the outward-opening type, the obvious is bound to happen – the plants will be sheared off and the scheme completely ruined.

Sash windows are the type best suited to the windowbox treatment; as you walk down the high street, just observe how those windowboxes which are full of bloom on the higher windowledges of shops and offices are showing off their absolute best.

rose attachment.

The correct watering of containers and baskets is as important as the correct compost. It is vital that they are regularly and thoroughly soaked, rather than constantly sprinkled with water. If good drainage has been provided, surplus water will quickly drain away and there will be no danger of rot through 'damping off'. If watered only lightly the plants produce roots just beneath the soil surface, and they are then vulnerable to hot sunshine and drying winds. It is not sufficient just to darken the surface of the compost – the surplus must be seen running out of the drainage holes at the base.

Hanging baskets dry out much more quickly than tubs and windowboxes, so avoid placing them in situations where they are exposed to the full sun or constant drying breezes.

A beautiful double white cultivar, Frank Unsworth, perfectly displayed in a container which allows the blooms to cascade downwards. Note the striking contrast with the red pelargonium

---

COMBINATIONS FOR CONTAINERS

Fuchsias are very versatile plants for container cultivation, associating well with a wide range of annual flowering and foliage subjects, which often appreciate the same moist compost conditions desired by fuchsias. (Avoid the Livingstone daisy, *Mesembryanthemum criniflorum*, and the modern gazania cultivars, which really need drier conditions.) Even geraniums, which are from hot spots in southern Africa, adapt well to the cooler, damper conditions which fuchsias find essential.

Some of the happiest combinations are of fuchsias and ivy-leafed geraniums, the fuchsias providing plants of an upright habit and the geraniums a scrambling skirt. Ivy-leafed geraniums are available in a wide colour range, and the latest, unusual, seed-raised strains present interesting possibilities. However, it is amongst the vegetatively propagated kinds that most gardeners make their selection. We are particularly enamoured with the rich purple-and-white flowered Harlequin and the lovely cream and grey-green, variegated-foliage cultivar L'Elegante. These provide a lovely foil for fuchsias like Margaret Roe or Bernadette when growing in a sizeable tub. Do not mix your fuchsia or geranium cultivars. Go instead for a double combination – two varieties strongly represented have much more impact than eight or ten mixed plants.

In our opinion, French marigolds and fuchsias do not rest easily in the same container, but the fact remains that many gardeners combine these plants to startling effect. If this brilliance of colour is to your taste, then select only modern FI hybrids that have proved themselves in our climate. The best way to find out about these is to look at the recommendations of the Fleuroselect organisation. This is a European body which trials flower seeds extensively throughout Europe and makes awards to those that perform creditably everywhere. Queen Bee is unquestionably the best French marigold, and it associates admirably with most fuchsia cultivars.

Looking after the Container or Basket

Whether it be a planter, windowbox or hanging basket, dead and dying flowers and foliage must be regularly removed. The removal of faded blooms ensures continuity of flowering. Trailing fuchsias always require manicuring, or they begin to look rank and unsightly. Regular pinching back of extension growths in the early part of the season will ensure that laterals are produced for more cover.

It is also important to remember that with such a restricted root run regular feeding will be important, and compost in all containers, irrespective of size, will need changing completely every season. Watch for pests and diseases, and spray regularly with a systemic insecticide containing dimeothate and a systemic fungicide in which the active ingredient is benomyl. This will ensure good clean stock.

As fuchsias grown in containers and baskets are unlikely to survive the winter outside, even if of the hardy varieties, it is necessary to remove and store them through the winter. This operation is exactly the same as that recommended for the greenhouse grower and exhibitor, the loft or attic being perfectly adequate accommodation for the most sophisticated cultivars providing that they are properly prepared for their winter vigil (for details of overwintering see Chapter 4).

FUCHSIAS AS HOUSEPLANTS

All experienced fuchsia growers would agree that the home is not the best place to grow fuchsias. However, it is where most enthusiasms for the plant begin and so we must consider the possibilities. The problem is our modern lifestyle of high temperatures and a dry atmosphere – it is in the sunny windows of old, cool, and often damp farmhouses and country cottages that the best indoor fuchsias are always seen.

The older cultivars (see individual descriptions in Chapter 10) tend to perform more satisfactorily in the home than the latest exhibition kinds. Indeed, most commercial cultivars that are widely available from general nurseries and garden centres during spring and summer are likely to be suitable, for it is these that are considered to be the easiest and most prolific.

When choosing fuchsias for the home, bear in mind their ultimate size. Often the best houseplants develop from dwarf cultivars like Tom Thumb and Lady Thumb, which are short-jointed, free-flowering and of neat, compact habit. Pendant varieties are not suitable unless grown in hanging pots, and even then it is difficult to keep a balanced habit given the uneven light dispersal in the average living room. They can also become rather unwieldy if grown in pots in the conventional fashion.

The key to success with fuchsias as houseplants is to provide them with as cool and humid an atmosphere as possible. This can be provided by standing the pots on a tray or large pan of gravel filled to the top of the gravel with water. Alternatively, stand each plant in a separate pot or container and pack around them with damp green sphagnum moss or coarse peat. The latter method provides the easiest means of exercising control over potential waterlogging, and permits the use of decorative containers which are functional too. Both methods create cool, damp micro-climates around each plant and help them to grow well in an otherwise unfriendly environment.

Light is very important too, for in most houses the ratio of warmth to light, especially during spring and autumn, is completely out of proportion. High temperatures and poor light result in drawn plants with pale foliage and wide spaces between their leaves. Fuchsias generally dislike high temperatures as they mostly originate from species which naturally grow in the cool, damp, elevated regions of South America. Treat them essentially as cool house plants, even though they may be somewhat tropical and exotic in appearance.

Good light does not mean that they enjoy standing in a hot, sunny, south-facing window, although sun-

A pot-grown fuchsia for the house, packed in moist peat

shine for at least a good part of the day is desirable. The full glare of the sun through a window is likely to cause scorching and drying of the foliage, together with 'spotting' if droplets of water remain on the leaves and the sun shines through. Drops of water serve as magnifying glasses and bright sun causes scorching of the tissue beneath, often followed by secondary fungal infections that give the plant an unpleasant, spotty appearance. Foliage damaged in this way survives rather than recovers, remaining unsightly until the end of the season, and this can happen even when the sun is only moderately fierce so take care to avoid splashing the foliage.

It is best to introduce to the house plants that are just at the stage of developing buds – those tiny pinhead buds in the axils of the leaves. Such plants become acclimatised more successfully than others to life in the home and, if grown until full-bud size, are less likely to

What a trio! Ideally placed in a patio corner, a standard of Meike Meursing provides a contrast in height with pots of the brightly variegated Gold Runner, and the beautiful all-red cascade fuchsia Red Spider

---

PATIO SCHEMES

The planting of fuchsias in a patio scheme is wide open to the imagination, depending on the size of the patio in question – it may need or be suitable for only the larger fuchsia standards planted in big pots, which are strategically placed here and there.

Today more and more 'patios' are being built onto houses both old and new. Many are the enclosed conservatory type, and anything grown in these must be treated as being grown in a greenhouse, but the ideal setting for fuchsias is on an open patio with perhaps just a roof above it (try the car port in summer). The fresh open air treatment and overhead shelter give the fuchsias ideal living conditions.

As for containers, the choice is huge: from expensive stone urns and other decorative containers to the cheaper plastic tubs, pots and plant holders. A mixture of fuchsias and geraniums are perhaps at their best in the old fashioned urn-type container – fuchsias surrounded with orange tagetes and a few trailing plants make a good alternative.

A hanging basket could be suspended from the patio roof and will again be well protected from the inclement weather (half or wall baskets are at their best in this sort of situation). Using either all fuchsias or a mixture of fuchsias, geraniums, begonias, nasturtiums, trailing lobelia and busy lizzie, a magnificent display of colourful bloom can be held until the end of September. A full or half basket, or indeed any hanging container which is full of plants, will require watering at least once a day – twice in really hot weather – so sensible placing to suit the person who has to tend the plants must always be borne in mind. It is also very advantageous to give an occasional overhead spray of fresh water, and a foliar feed is something for which any plant will be grateful.

suffer from bud or flower drop. This is a common problem with fuchsias purchased in full flower and brought into the house. Sometimes it is the abrupt change of environment that causes it – the transition from comfortable light, humid greenhouse to dry, hot living room, often with a spell on a draughty market stall or florist's shopfront in between, is understandably too much. The first reaction of such a plant in its quest for survival is to drop its blossoms. It will eventually recover, but the rehabilitation may take several weeks.

Watering and Composts
There are three main watering problems. These are overwatering, underwatering, or just irregular watering, and they are often caused by using the wrong compost rather than by the hand of the gardener with the watering can. The subtleties of various composts will be discussed later (see Chapter 4), but suffice it to say at present that there are two main types – soil-less and soil-based. Those referred to as soil-less consist of peat, or peat and sand, and have a balance of nutrients added. The soil-based kinds are dominated by the John Innes composts, the most consistent and reliable of those with a significant soil content. John Innes composts are available in several forms, but mainly consist of peat, sand and loam – the latter a somewhat mythical soil which is fibrous and midway between a sandy soil and heavy clay. Both soil-less and soil-based composts can serve the same purpose, but require slightly different treatment to achieve success.

Soil-less composts are quick acting, light, and easy to handle, young plants advancing well in all respects. For longer-term fuchsia culture these composts are useful too, for fuchsias require regular repotting (see below) and the medium should not deteriorate significantly during the relatively short period between replacement. It should be remembered, though, that the peat in such compost is an organic material that eventually decomposes, the process being hastened by regular feeding with liquid houseplant feeds. With peat forming the entire, or majority, of the bulk of the compost, this decomposition can create problems if repotting is not regularly undertaken. Apart from the hostile, airless conditions which then develop in the compost and restrict proper root development, mosses and liverworts invade the surface and sciarid flies (see Chapter 11) take up residence. Although they are predominantly consumers of decomposing organic matter, the presence of the latter, together with the general anaerobic conditions within the compost, can quickly lead to the widespread death of vital nutrient-transmitting root hairs.

Soil-based composts, on the other hand, while not yielding such rapid results or bushy growth, do offer the indoor fuchsia grower more stability. Watering is easier to get right with a compost with a significant proportion of soil, this also acting as a buffer against the breakdown caused by regular liquid feeding. The presence of soil in a compost allows for a greater margin of error when watering, for it permits the percolation of surplus moisture through the compost much more rapidly than if it were made up entirely of moisture-retaining peat. Indeed, it is the excessive moisture-holding capacity of peat, together with the relative difficulty of wetting it when it has been allowed to dry out, that makes soil-less composts less popular with beginners to fuchsia growing. John Innes Potting Compost No 2 is recommended for all actively growing plants in the home.

Whenever possible use clay pots. Not that these are any better for the plants, but it is well known that the moisture content of the compost in a clay pot can be more easily recognised than when confined by a plastic pot. Take a short length of dowel rod or a stick of similar substance and tap the pot. If a dull thud results the compost is damp, if a ringing sound is heard, then it is dry. With John Innes compost and clay pots, fuchsia cultivation in the home is somewhat eased, providing that repotting takes place regularly.

Above:
Marinka is an all-red fuchsia which is, fortunately, often seen where it belongs – in a hanging pot or basket. It is one to be grown indoors, as when the weather is cold the leaves will turn reddish-purple outside

Right:
Derby Imp, displayed exactly as it should be – so that you look up into the flowers

Repotting

This often causes consternation to the newcomer to greenhouse gardening, for there is believed to be a certain mystique surrounding the operation and people are unsure as to when to perform it. It is obviously better to repot a plant just before it needs it, but the novice fuchsia grower may have difficulty in recognising just when that is, so many fuchsias are allowed to go beyond that point and then they will start to deteriorate. A general gauntness and paleness of foliage, often accompanied by sparse flower production, is the overall aspect of a fuchsia that is in need of repotting. The rootball will be woody and congested, often with roots pushing out through the drainage

Growing in a stone urn is that glorious red-and-white cultivar, Celia Smedley. Here it forms a lively backcloth to variegated and green-leaved pelargoniums – a blue trailing lobelia completes the picture

holes of the pot. The compost surface will probably have a stale look about it, heightened by the presence of mosses or liverworts. When repotted, most fuchsias will rapidly recover from any abuse, but it is better to catch them before they go into decline so that strong healthy growth can continue unchecked.

During the active growing period do not be frightened to turn a plant out of its pot and inspect the rootball. There is no need to poke it about, but a regular inspection will indicate whether everything is in good order. Do not pay too much regard to the concentrated presence of roots towards the sides of the pot, for it is quite natural for them to gravitate there and is not necessarily an indication that the plant must be repotted. Similarly, roots that push through the drainage holes may not always indicate congestion within the pot, for if the pot has been standing on a gravel tray in moist conditions it is quite normal for adventurous roots to probe around outside. The best way to tell whether a plant needs repotting is to squeeze the compost with your fingers. If there is any 'give' in the compost it shows that it has not been completely ramified by roots and therefore nothing need yet be done. If the compost feels hard and solid, then clearly repotting is a matter of priority.

When repotting, ensure that there is adequate drainage in the bottom of the pot. A generous layer of small pea gravel or broken crocks over the drainage holes in clay pots should be adequate if one of the standard proprietary brands of potting compost is to be used. Remove the plant to be repotted from its pot by inverting it and giving the top rim of the pot a sharp downward blow on the potting bench. If the rootball is very congested, run a knife down it in two or three places to allow fresh roots to break out. If the rootball is not tightly congested and just firm, then leave it undisturbed. The plant should be centred in its new pot (see diagram) and the compost gently firmed down with the fingers – never the thumbs as this gives uneven pressure – between the old rootball and the edge of the

Repotting into a larger pot

pot. There should be room down the side of the pot between the rootball and the pot wall to allow you to do this – a pot one size up on the previous one will be about right. Lightly top off the compost, allowing 1cm (⅓in) from the top of the pot to the compost for watering. If you are using a John Innes potting compost, then the compost must be firmed before watering. When a soil-less kind is utilised, fill the pot with compost to the rim and water, allowing the watering to settle it down rather than firming it with your fingers. Soil-less compost that is packed tightly is devoid of air and virtually impervious to water, especially if the surface layer is permitted to dry out.

Routine Care

Once the compost is in good order (see Repotting above), watering becomes less hazardous and the indoor fuchsia has an excellent opportunity to prosper, given cool, humid conditions with plenty of light. Little else need be done to keep such a plant in good order, providing that a regular spraying regime against the inevitable aphids and other assailants that delight in preying upon succulent fuchsia foliage is maintained. The relatively few horrors that trouble the fuchsia grower are investigated elsewhere (see Chapter 11), but the average home fuchsia grower can control most of the common pests with a regular houseplant insecticide spray. Red spider mite can still be troublesome despite this, but humid conditions should prevent its appearance. Fungal diseases are rarely troublesome on actively growing indoor fuchsias. Mildew occasionally manifests itself as a white deposit on the foliage, and when this happens you should stand the affected plants outside for a few days and spray with a systemic fungicide in which the active ingredient is benomyl.

Apart from these problems, the main concern of the indoor fuchsia grower should be hygiene. As flowers and leaves fade they should be removed. Do not allow old blossoms to cling to the branches, nor shed leaves to accumulate on the surface of the pot. Both are capable of harbouring pests and diseases. Turn the pot regularly so that each side faces the window for a period: this ensures that there is even foliage development, resulting in a shapely plant which is not so likely to drop its foliage prematurely. Leaves on the room side of a plant grown on a windowledge have a much shorter life than those provided with as much light as possible. A quarter turn of the pot daily is sufficient.

Keeping the foliage in good condition also depends upon regular feeding. Fuchsias are hungry plants and quickly deplete the available nutrients in proprietary potting composts. Straightforward houseplant liquid feeds are perfectly adequate if administered at about fortnightly intervals throughout the active growing period. Regular feeding fosters lusty growth and good flower production. However, the growth that results is not always as even as one would like, so regular pinching back to provide a balanced framework is essential.

Treat fuchsias being grown as houseplants in the same way as those prepared for the show bench, utilising the same pleasing training arrangements (see Chapter 5) as advocated for the exhibitor. It is this attention to detail which leads to success, which in turn can be an encouragement to the indoor fuchsia grower to take his or her hobby further and become an exhibitor.

Where better to use this basket cultivar, Jack Shahan, than in a container placed in the top of an old chimney pot, here in the garden of one of our photographers, Enid Pyrah. With the pale fronds of a fern in front and leaves turning colour behind, this is a good example of what can be achieved in the early autumn garden

4
Advanced Care and Cultivation

This chapter is written with the greenhouse-owning exhibitor in mind, but much of it is also applicable to the gardener who just wishes to improve his fuchsias. The care and cultivation of fuchsias is generally much more successful if you have access to a greenhouse and, if you wish to advance to exhibiting your plants, the versatility which this provides is essential.

GREENHOUSES AND FRAMES

Choosing the Greenhouse
If you are in the fortunate position of being able to choose a greenhouse in which to grow your fuchsias you are a good way towards achieving their successful cultivation, for the structure which is selected can have a profound effect upon the results achieved and the cultural methods which can be employed. Greenhouses are available in all manner of shapes and sizes, and take forms that vary from the conservatory and sunlounge to the enclosed porch around the front door. All are very useful and can accommodate a surprisingly large number of fuchsias. However, a properly constructed greenhouse is the easiest to manage and best suited to fuchsia cultivation.

Modern greenhouses come in four basic forms: the lean-to, in which one wall is formed by the dwelling-house or other substantial building; the span-roof type, which is built on a dwarf wall and has a pitched roof; the Dutch light kind, formerly constructed of Dutch lights but in the modern form a glass-to-ground greenhouse; and the hexagonal type that is broadly speaking dome-shaped, but with angular sides. All have their advocates, but it is generally conceded that where there is ample space a span-roof type is the most versatile choice.

Staging (benching) should be provided at waist height down either side, and a shelf near the roof ridge is handy if this can be kept above head height. Ventilation must be adequate, and most growers agree that both side and ridge ventilators are essential. A good wide door is necessary for easy management, wide enough to take a wheelbarrow without skinning your fingers and with no tiresome step or ramp. Heating is desirable, but may be prohibitively expensive. If you cannot afford to heat your greenhouse, then consider investing in either a small propagator or a heated bench. Both are extremely useful.

Greenhouses can be constructed of many different materials. Polythene houses are cheap to purchase initially, but need re-covering every two years and in winter will often suffer wind or snow damage. They are well known for their ability to gather condensation in seemingly disproportionate quantities to any other structure, and for this reason too they are rarely favoured by fuchsia growers. Those made of corrugated perspex are little better, cracking and discolouring with the weather. Glass is obviously the most satisfactory material to use, but the most suitable kind of framework is more difficult to decide upon. Cedar and teak that are kept well oiled are obviously ideal, but are extremely expensive, while ordinary softwood painted in white looks good but has a very limited life. Aluminium would seem to be the best answer as it does not rust, but in some cases the bolts and screws that hold it together are steel and liable to corrode. So inspect any intended purchase of this kind very carefully.

The Garden Frame

A frame is as invaluable to a fuchsia grower as a greenhouse in its own small way. The fact that you have a greenhouse does not mean that a frame is unnecessary. It is in all probability *more* essential as it provides a halfway house between the greenhouse and open ground, enabling plants to be hardened off gently before being planted out. Plants removed directly from greenhouse to garden usually suffer a check in growth, are often badly chilled, and take several weeks to recover.

There are nearly as many designs for frames as there are for greenhouses, and while the pitch-roofed kind is likely to be the most useful, the traditional Dutch-light type has much to commend it.

Basic Management

Detailed management instructions will be provided in due course (see below), but in the meantime it is profitable to mention some of the general rules of good greenhouse management.

•Regular watering may seem to be an obvious instruction, but it is surprising how many gardeners water only when the plants are already suffering from lack of water, to the certain detriment of the plants. Watering should be frequent, with monitoring of the compost to ensure the correct amount. Good, stable growth can never be achieved by irregular watering.

•A humid atmosphere is beneficial, especially during the summer months, so regularly spraying the path and gravel under the benches helps in this respect. Avoid getting water on to the foliage of plants during hot sunny weather – the droplets of water serve as small magnifying glasses during bright weather and the tissue beneath becomes scorched.

•During the late spring and peak summer period the greenhouse must be provided with some kind of shading. Roller blinds are expensive but good, although most of the sun-shade products that are mixed with water and applied with a brush are equally functional,

if not as visually pleasing.

•Ventilation should be given freely during warm weather and moderately during cooler periods. The free circulation of air amongst plants helps to reduce the incidence of fungal diseases like botrytis.

•During the duller days of winter and early spring ensure that maximum light is admitted to the greenhouse. Clean the glass in the autumn and then again during early spring.

•Cleanliness is important in all parts of the structure if pests and diseases are to be successfully controlled. A thorough cleansing of rafters, brickwork and other fixtures with a solution of potassium permanganate and water, or a heavy disinfectant like Jeyes Fluid, immediately before plants from the garden are returned indoors will pay dividends. Dead leaves and

Allan's greenhouse. At flowering time the plants have put on maximum growth and the greenhouse is overflowing with a riot of colour and contrast. At this time of year shading and full ventilation are imperative

discarded plants should be disposed of regularly and not allowed to accumulate beneath the staging to harbour pests and diseases. Regular cleaning and maintenance results in healthy plants and a trouble-free structure in which to produce them. Cleanliness is equally important in a frame.

CULTIVATION

The start of the growing season depends very much upon whether you have a heated greenhouse. If you do, then some plants can be kept growing throughout the winter. (If not, then plants must be overwintered (see below) in their dormant state, not returning to the greenhouse until spring.) Cuttings for small pot culture are usually taken during early spring, so in the heated greenhouse a variety of plant material in different stages of growth is likely to be present for much of the year. This should not greatly affect management, for all stages of actively growing plant have the same temperature and humidity requirements.

Temperature and Heating

A high temperature is not desirable, for the species from which most modern fuchsia cultivars have been derived, although originating in South America, come from cool, damp regions of high elevation. During the growing period a minimum night temperature of 7.5°C (45°F) will ensure survival and unchecked growth, although a minimum of 10°C (50°F) is better and will assist with the development and cultivation of show cultivars that are tied to a rigid schedule. Ideally, day temperatures should not go above 15-18°C (60-65°F). In practice, it is likely that they will exceed this by several degrees in hot weather, for despite constant shading and damping down it is impossible to make sufficient reductions in temperature within the confines of a small domestic greenhouse. When temperatures soar, provide as much ventilation and shading as possible, and damp down regularly by spraying clear water on the floor, and especially the path, taking care not to get any splashes on the foliage where they are likely to cause sun scorch.

If you have a choice of heating, then purchase an electrical fan-type heater. Not only does this provide warmth, but it also circulates the air on muggy autumn days, although it is costly. In the summer it can also be switched to the cool air position to reduce high temperatures. Gas and paraffin heaters are not as desirable, as they produce a damp heat and do not readily circulate the air.

If you can afford to heat your greenhouse, it also makes sense to insulate it to minimise heat loss. There are many methods of doing this, but the clear plastic bubble insulation material now available is simple to fix and rarely causes any problems with condensation. Clear polythene has always been considered to be the most suitable insulation, causing minimal reduction in light and trapping a barrier of air between. It has, however, always been associated with condensation, a buildup of light-reducing algae, and a fragility which is not so evident in modern clear bubble insulation. Whether you go for the bubble insulation or traditional polythene, it is important to provide for the opening of ventilators when fastening it to the internal structure of the greenhouse. Insulation may well still be useful at night during spring, but on sunny days the temperature will rocket and full ventilation may be necessary.

A balance between air circulation and humidity is as important to the successful culture of fuchsias as a steady temperature. A greenhouse with both ridge and side vents is ideal, the louvred kind of wall ventilators being extremely useful. A louvred window fitted in the opposite end to the door will provide a much needed through draught in high summer. Slatted staging is generally to be preferred to help the free circulation of air, but the necessary humidity can be obtained with solid staging if the plants are placed directly onto constantly damp gravel. Similar results can be achieved if the greenhouse floor is soil, with a generous covering of gravel that is periodically sprayed with water. Ventilate whenever possible during the main growing season, and keep the air moist during warm weather. Conversely, during early spring and autumn the atmosphere should be drier than that outside.

Summer

Plants that are not intended for showing can be placed outside when all danger of frost has passed. (The ideal period for this operation is around the end of the second week in June.) Whenever possible, plunge the pots in a bed of peat, sand, or ashes to keep the roots cool, but take care that the plants are potted on regularly. Plunging means that they are less likely to show any signs of requiring repotting, for the roots will rapidly spread out through the drainage holes of the

This is Royal Velvet, one of the large, double-flowered cultivars from the USA, which are not to everyone's taste. A fast-growing plant which, due to the size and weight of the blooms, will need staking if grown as a bush

Below:
Billy Green, a self-pink triphylla cultivar, and probably the best of its colour. Like all triphylla types, it enjoys warmth and a hot summer, when it can be placed outside to revel in full sun

pots into the surrounding medium. A few emerging roots will do no harm, but a large mat of them has to be cut off before re-potting, to the subsequent detriment of the plant, or the pot has to be smashed in order to remove them.

All fuchsias benefit from being outside during the summer, but as show date approaches it is unwise to allow exhibition plants to take their chance with the vagaries of the weather and the predations of slugs. Take show plants in well before the date so that they can be properly prepared.

Pests and Diseases

Pests and diseases are a constant threat to fuchsias, so it is prudent to spray regularly from bud burst until leaf fall with both a systemic fungicide and systemic insecticide. If you are exhibiting, a greenhouse smoke is a better proposition around show time than a liquid spray, as it does not pose any risk to flowers or foliage. Again, bees sometimes damage blossoms, so prior to the show date cover the door and ventilator openings with fine net curtaining to prevent entry. This will only stop large flying insects: smaller ones like aphids will always find their way in. Awareness of pests and diseases is vital throughout the growing season, specific problems being addressed in detail later in the book (see Chapter 11).

COMPOSTS

A plant reflects in its growth and general condition the quality of the compost in which it is growing. In the last chapter we stressed the importance of a good, well-balanced compost when growing plants for the home and this is even more important when perfection is sought with a show specimen. The mysteries of Allan's success as a showman will be revealed presently (see below), but initially we should consider the standard composts that are available, for without question these are the best to begin with. Variations can be made when experience has been gained.

Soil-based composts

Soil-based composts are predominantly John Innes types, mixtures of loam, peat and sand with nutrients added in various quantities. There are three strengths – John Innes No 1, No 2 and No 3. No 1 is used for plants which are going to spend a short period in the same pot, No 2 is for those that will remain in a pot for a whole season, while No 3 is for longer-term plants. Typically, this latter is the compost used for semi-permanent houseplants like the rubber plant and parlour palm.

John Innes composts have a specific formula which is well known, but which we will not seek to repeat here for fear of encouraging the gardener to mix his own. The major problem with attempting to make your own John Innes composts is the main component – sterilised loam. A good loam soil is difficult to come by, and for most gardeners it is impossible to sterilise successfully in small quantities. The correct temperature for successful 'sterilisation' kills the undesirable pathogens and weed seeds, but permits the desirable soil micro-organisms to remain. The measurements of volume used when adding plant foods to the mix are bushels, and who today has a bushel box, or even knows what one looks like? John Innes composts should be left in the hands of the professionals, those who belong to the John Innes Manufacturers' Association. Seek bags of compost with their kite mark and you will not be disappointed.

Soil-less composts

Soil-less composts come in many and varied combinations and it is difficult to judge which is the best. Growers have their own preferences, often adapting the composts to their own needs. There are two main kinds – the peat and sand mix, and the straight peat compost. The former is typified by Arthur Bower's compost, the latter by Levington compost. There are other equally good branded products in each classification, as well as recommendations for mixing your own using a peat base. Unlike John Innes composts, soil-less kinds are a good proposition to mix for yourself if you have the time and patience. If you do not, or are unsure what you are trying to achieve, then stay with a good branded product.

Compost Recommendations and Making your Own
Top exhibition growers have their own ideas about what the compost should be, so when an opportunity arises to discover what they do, grasp it with both hands. The following compost recommendations are based upon the success of Allan as an exhibitor. They are not the only way of achieving prizewinning standards, but they are a valuable guide for the new showman as to what can be done to improve the quality of growth.

While a soil-based compost has the benefit of living microbes working within it, there are disadvantages for the advanced grower or exhibitor which usually lead him to using a soil-less medium. The heavy weight of John Innes and the variation in quality of the loam used can cause difficulty, so a good compost for exhibition fuchsias is frequently based upon a soil-less compost with several additives.

In the plants' formative life a wholly organically-based compost is used. For rooted cuttings and for repotting, Cowpost is used without additives. This is a compost made from specially treated cow dung, peat and perlite. This latter material is white, granular, and derived from a specially treated crushed rock. When mixed into a compost it confers excellent moisture-retaining qualities.

Plants that are to receive their final potting are grown in a different mixture:

⅔ by volume Arthur Bower's
    Seed and Potting Compost
½ by volume medium-grade perlite
4 double handfuls Cowpact
1 handful bonemeal
1 handful fishmeal

An excellent white double, tinged pink, Harry Gray is easy to grow and self-branching. This is an ideal plant for anyone – expert and beginner alike – wishing to produce a floriferous hanging pot or basket display

This is a very rough-and-ready analysis, for not all handfuls are the same size, but where common sense prevails a most satisfactory compost can be made. The volume measurements for compost and perlite are based upon the use of an 18 litre (4 gal) bucket. The use of Cowpact encourages the rapid development of desirable micro-organisms in the compost. It is made from pure cow manure and is quite safe for pot-grown plants, unlike horse and poultry manure, which often have a high ammonia concentration and scorch the roots of pot-grown plants.

Another mixture which has been used very successfully recently is:

½ by volume Humber soil-less potting compost
¼ by volume John Innes Potting Compost No 2
¼ by volume medium-grade perlite

Once again this is based upon the use of an 18 litre (4 gal) bucket, to which is added:

4 large double handfuls Cowpact
2 large double handfuls arcillite
1 handful calcified seaweed.

This is less well tried than the previous mixture, but is currently giving much better results.

Lime is an important constituent of any compost. Acidity or alkalinity in a compost is measured on the pH scale. Above pH7 is alkaline, below is acid. Most fuchsias require a pH of 6.6. However, it is not vital to their development to be absolutely exact. Although the optimum is pH6.6, fuchsias will grow satisfactorily to several factors either way. They are not fastidious, but for the best results the pH of both the compost and water needs careful monitoring. Modern test kits, and more especially pH meters, are quite accurate enough.

Look out for increasing levels of acidity as the summer progresses. Heavy feeding tends to acidify the compost very quickly. Watch for this happening, and as a precaution water your plants during midsummer with a lime solution. Use ordinary garden lime and mix one tablespoonful in 9 litres (2 gal) of water. Mix it at least twenty-four hours before you need it, to ensure that it causes no damage.

Whatever compost you decide to use at the beginning, do experiment. This is one of the most exciting and interesting projects that even the amateur can try for himself. A garden changes every year no matter what, but in the greenhouse the same composts can be

---

USING TREE BARK

One of the most recent introductions to the horticultural world has been the use of tree bark. It is available in a chipped or rough form that is used for mulching garden beds to keep moisture in and weeds down, with the added attraction of the ornamental value it gives to an area. It can be expensive if a large area is being covered, but it is well worthwhile. Bark is also available in a shredded or pulverised form, which is dug into the soil. It has the dual effect of helping the soil to retain moisture *and* to drain excess water away. In clay soils its incorporation aids the aeration and drainage of the soil, whilst in lighter, sandy soils it helps to hold together the fine particles by its action as humus, so helping the soil to hold moisture.

For the first time Allan has incorporated it into his potting compost, rightly or wrongly. Perlite has become so expensive that an alternative had to be found.

The mixture is:

½ bag of Humber Compost
½ bag of Calval John Innes No 2 Compost
¼ bag of Cowpact
¼ bag of ICI Pulverised Forest Bark

When mixed together the grist (texture) is beautiful, the smell of the compost mixture distinctly earthy. The smell of a compost is very important as it tells you something about it, but unfortunately it is something you cannot describe. One has only to say to someone 'Just smell this' and they will think you are mad! There have been warnings on the use of bark in potting compost, and as yet we have not seen it advocated for this use. Is the bark always from the same type of tree? Is it mixed? Will it vary from year to year? Will the mixture form a mould from the wood spores? All this has yet to be proved. So far, however, so good. Everything growing in it, all fuchsias, geraniums, and pelargoniums, are in top form.

Some very interesting reading can be found in *Fuchsias for all Purposes* (Country Life Ltd, 1959) by the late Tom Thorne. He readily advocates the use of the brown crumbly material to be found in a bracken bed and states that this bracken peat is far and above the value of anything that is currently on the market. It is clean and odourless and helps produce a strong, well-formed, quick-growing plant with good green foliage and shapely, colourful blooms. He states that if identical cuttings from a parent plant were taken and one placed in an ordinary compost and one in a compost with bracken peat incorporated, the plants being fed and watered in the same way, then the one grown in the bracken-incorporated compost appeared to be of a different or much improved cultivar.

used year in, year out. If things are growing well then leave well alone, but if not, do experiment. There is nothing to lose, and perhaps a lot to be gained!

FEEDING

Fuchsias are heavy feeders, and the grower must pay careful attention to this. Plants have different requirements each season and this should be reflected in the content of the feed. The main plant foods are nitrogen (N), phosphorus (P) and potassium (K). They are available to plants in the form of nitrates, phosphates and potash, their functions being the promotion of: foliage; a good root system; and flowers, fruit, and the ripening of wood, respectively. Trace elements are necessary too, but all good composts and most feeds have sufficient to prevent trace element deficiency, although it is wise to check that this is so. The only exception is that when a high potash feed is given a magnesium deficiency manifests itself, the foliage taking on a sickly yellow appearance. Epsom salts used as a foliar spray at the rate of 100g (4oz) in 13.5 litres (3 gal) of water rapidly corrects the problem.

Proprietary feeds are the best. Homemade feeds, like many homemade composts, are difficult to get right. For the spring, choose a feed with an analysis that is about N25%, P15%, K15%. For the summer change to N15%, P15%, K25%. The percentage figures should be given in an analysis on the packaging of the product and refer to the percentage of nitrate, phosphate and potash available to the plants. Spring feeding starts as soon as growth breaks away strongly, with the summer regime commencing the moment pinhead buds are spotted in the axils of the leaves. Some growers compromise with an N20%, P20%, K20% feed throughout spring and summer and this too can produce good results, especially if you are unsure of exactly when to switch feeds.

Foliar feeding can also be given, using any of the regular proprietary brands. Not only do plants absorb food through their roots, but liquid fertilisers sprayed

Beacon Rosa, one of the favourites in Allan's collection – he particularly likes the deeper pink colouring at the sepal tips. At its best when grown in a 15cm (6in) pot, it likes plenty of room, but repays any trouble taken with flowers, flowers and more flowers

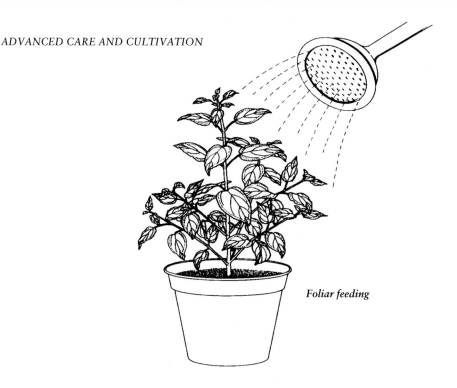

Foliar feeding

onto their leaves are also absorbed and utilised by the plants within a few hours. Feeding through the soil, particularly under dry, cold or waterlogged conditions, is slow and wasteful, whilst feeding through the leaves is rapid, efficient and less wasteful, as the plant is able to make almost full use of the fertiliser.

Foliar feeding involves wetting the foliage with a fine spray, ensuring that the spray lance gets right to the centre of each plant. To make sure that the feed sticks on the leaf for sufficient time to be successfully absorbed, mix in a couple of drops of liquid soap: this will prevent the spray from running off the foliage immediately after it has been applied.

An important factor to consider when foliar feeding is that it must never be done in bright sunlight, or scorching of the leaves will occur. The best time is in the very early morning before the rays of the sun become too hot. Alternatively it can be carried out in the evening, again when the heat has gone out of the sun. Try to avoid foliar spraying in the very late autumn or winter. If the atmosphere is cold and wet botrytis and rot will kill the plants.

Foliar feeding is not really a substitute for regular feeding with the watering, but is a useful adjunct to it. How much of each is applied, and when, is a personal decision which should be guided by the instructions provided with the product, and developed in the light of personal experience with specific cultivars.

POTTING

There is little difference between potting and repotting. The latter we discussed in the last chapter when considering fuchsias as houseplants. Potting itself is primarily undertaken for young rooted cuttings and for plants lifted from the garden to be brought in for the winter. As neither has a rootball, they must have a pot big enough to accommodate the existing root system, and in keeping with the size of the aerial parts of the plant. One of the most common errors in potting a young rooted cutting for the first time is to put it into too large a pot, with the idea that it will not require repotting too regularly. This is a grave mistake, for what usually happens is that the large body of compost around the plant becomes wet and stale. The young roots come into contact with this and then struggle or die back.

When placed in the pot, the plant should be held firmly and the compost gently poured around the roots. The young plant should be at the same level in the compost as it was in the propagator or ground. Do not firm the compost down, even if you are using a soil-based kind, but allow the first watering to settle it.

OVERWINTERING

The majority of gardeners who grow fuchsias have to prepare their plants for a dormant winter vigil. There are exceptions though, and experienced growers who have a heated greenhouse often grow on a proportion of their plants through the winter. These are usually the ones being grown on the so-called 'biennial' system.

Cuttings that were taken during late spring and early summer are progressively potted on, trained (see next chapter) and de-blossomed, being allowed to grow slowly but steadily through the winter. Watering is carefully controlled and the compost is kept just damp. Only occasional feeding at a half to a quarter strength should be allowed and an eye must be kept open for fungal diseases like botrytis, especially during periods where ventilating is difficult. The plants move into their final pots as winter gives way to spring. When exhibiting, the ideal situation is to have the final potting five months before show date. This allows the plants to fill the pots with roots and encourages a first-class floral display. *Never* pot on after the final pinch of the stems.

For the majority of fuchsia growers this method of cultivation is out of the question. At least it is for most of their plants, even if they have a heated greenhouse — it is much more economical to store plants in their dormant state in a cool, frost-free place than to spend money on heating for little tangible benefit. This is certainly the best method of overwintering fuchsias that have been used for bedding outside, for these have to be lifted and cleaned up for the winter in any event. Preparing them for dormant winter storage at the same time is not only simple, but space saving and economical, as well as being the only way in which a gardener with no greenhouse at all can hope to save any stock for the following year.

Preparation

However, winter storage does not begin with the lifting of fuchsias from outside or the gradual withdrawal of water from those inside. It begins some time before then, usually late summer, especially for those grown unfettered in open ground. A feed or two of potash to replace the more balanced diet previously administered not only helps to bring out the best in the blossoms, but also toughens up the wood. This is particularly necessary after a wet summer where luxu-

Golden Marinka – not the easiest of fuchsias, but a fantastic sight when well grown. Seen here in combination with ivy-leaved pelargoniums and petunias in a hanging basket, it is also superb when grown as a full basket on its own

riant growth has been made. Slowly withdrawing water from those in pots, whether outside or under glass, has a similar effect, the wood ripening more satisfactorily than if watering continues as normal. It is vital that the wood hardens reasonably well if excessive dieback is to be avoided during the winter.

Ripe wood is not the only criterion for successful storage: absence of foliage and a clear break of the leaf stalk or petiole from the stem is essential if fungal infections, and subsequent dieback, are to be avoided. Removing foliage before it is ready to part naturally is a hazardous business, as the leaf scar is open tissue and very vulnerable to infection. Plants have to be persuaded to defoliate naturally, either by withdrawing moisture or allowing frosting. For indoor plants the former is clearly appropriate, but for outdoor plants and those standing outside in pots for the summer months there is nothing more satisfactory than a frost. Not just one, but possibly two or three. If the wood is properly ripened no harm will be done and, providing that the frost is not of sufficient severity to freeze the soil hard, then the roots will be quite safe. As with dahlias and summer-flowering bulbs, fuchsias lose their foliage cleanly following frosting, and the tissues appear to seal up and make fungal entry more difficult. A frosted fuchsia plant will have black hanging foliage, rather slimy and unpleasant to the touch. If the plant is moved into a cool dry place the leaves will become crisp and merely shake off the plant. It is important that before being placed in store all plants are free of any vestige of foliage, even if it is dry and crumbly. If allowed to remain it will almost certainly attract various fungal diseases and moulds.

When a plant has lost all its foliage the framework can clearly be seen. Often this looks untidy and unbalanced, and the natural tendency is to get the secateurs out and trim the offending branches back. For one or two of the larger plants this may be considered a necessity, but for the majority it is a hazardous operation at the very least. Cutting back often leads to bleeding and subsequent dieback problems, especially with fuchsias lifted from open ground where control over watering cannot be exercised. Even where the withdrawal of water has been practised in an effort to reduce sap flow, it is unwise to remove more than a third of the growth if fungal infections are to be avoided. When bleeding occurs from a cut branch and the flow is not stemmed quickly, then use charcoal dusted over the raw end to seal it. The most useful charcoal is that sold by pet shops as filter carbon for aquarium filters.

Storage

Once the fuchsias have been cleaned up and look just like fine, twiggy skeletons they are ready for storage. Indoor plants are already in pots and can be stored as they are. Bedding cultivars lifted from the open ground can be either potted or boxed in damp peat or potting compost. This should be drier (see below) than when used for potting. Standard fuchsias that are used as dot plants in bedding displays have often been planted in their pots and these can simply be lifted, but those that are not should be dug up carefully and potted in a good compost. (Unlike their bedding counterparts, standards are kept from year to year.)

Although fuchsias go dormant for the winter and the gardener can in many ways, from a horticultural point of view, prepare them better than nature can, they do not cease to function completely. They are slowly ticking over inside their woody framework and do require careful watching for water. Heavy watering is counter-productive, but extreme dryness will kill. Slightly dampened compost is perfect. It should never be allowed to dry out so much that the rootball pulls away from the inner edge of the pot, and never be so wet that when the surface is pressed with the finger, moisture is exuded.

Many places can be suitable for storing fuchsias, but the attic or loft are favourites – reasonably easily accessible, dry and cool, but unlikely to freeze. The plants

that are in pots are predominantly specimens of one kind or another, and need treating a little more carefully than those used for bedding or merely as stock plants for cuttings. These can be placed upright in boxes or pots – when brought into the light in spring the emerging shoots can be used for cuttings with which to start fresh plants, while the old stock material is scrapped. Pot-grown plants are a different proposition for almost all are trained, and therefore it is important that if the shape is to be maintained the buds should break evenly. There is a theory amongst exhibitors, largely taken from the practice of the glasshouse vine grower, that if the overwintered plants are laid in a horizontal plain the breaking of buds will be more even. We have not investigated the scientific reasons for this claim, but it is readily acknowledged by expert growers as being a reliable fact of life. Plants that have been lying on their side all winter and are then taken into the warmth seem to break more readily from lower down the stem than those which have been standing upright from the time that they were put away.

Apart from inspecting the plants regularly during the winter to ensure that they do not dry out completely nor become infected with fungal diseases, there is little to do. If a suitable storage place is chosen the plants can be put to the back of your mind, to leave you time to browse through the new catalogues.

There is one other method of storage which we should perhaps mention here, although neither of us can recommend it, especially on the cold uncompromising clay soil of Harrogate, and that is 'clamping'. This involves burying your fuchsias in the soil, rather like farmers do with potatoes. With the aid of a straw chimney, air is able to circulate and supposedly keep the plants in good health until the spring. What actually happens, unless you are both lucky and live on a light soil, is that the store becomes filled with water and the plants rot. Do not be tempted into this folly – the loft or attic is a much safer place.

Standard fuchsias provide height above pelargoniums in a greenhouse display at Crathes Castle, Scotland

5
Training

Irrespective of whether fuchsias are grown for home and garden decoration or for exhibition, they demand a certain amount of training. The ultimate extent of training that is desirable for exhibition plants is outlined here, but much of this is also relevant to the fuchsia on the window ledge, and those in tubs and borders in the garden. The plants will then achieve their full potential.

There are many shapes, sizes and configurations into which modern fuchsias can be trained, but all depend upon a good, sturdy, well-rooted cutting at the outset. It should have been taken from a lateral or terminal vegetative shoot (see Appendix 2) rather than a flowering one, be clean and healthy, and with short distances between leaf joints. Before training proper can commence the plant should be established in a pot of good-quality potting compost. At least two weeks should be allowed between potting and the commencement of training.

When training a fuchsia for showing, the exact dimensions given in Chapter 8 (Exhibiting) should be adhered to.

SHRUB
When taking a cutting that is intended to become a shrub, it is prudent to leave any small axillary buds (see Appendix 2) below compost level intact. These are potential branches from beneath soil level, although

they sometimes rot rather than develop. Once the cutting is well established in its pot it should be pinched back to two or four pairs of leaves. The exact number of leaves that you pinch back to depends upon the cultivar being used and the eventual size of plant that you require. There are no hard and fast rules, although it is generally acknowledged that a better-balanced plant results from consistently pinching to an equal number of leaf joints.

If, for example, a plant is selected and the growing point is pinched out at four pairs of leaves it will cease growing upwards, but start to produce lateral growths. When these newly formed branches have developed two pairs of leaves, then they should be pinched out again. Further similar growth will develop from the leaf axils. Every time shoots are pinched out, the branching potential of the plant is doubled, thereby improving potential flower yield. Four or five stops for

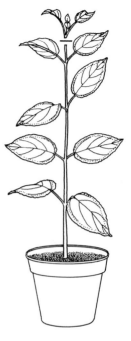

Above:
A cutting stopped at four pairs of leaves. This is the first stop required in the initial stage of shaping a shrub or bush plant

Left:
Further pinching out of the shoot tips will keep the plant in the uniform shape which is required for show bench work. It is important that all shoots are nipped out at the same time

most cultivars will yield a satisfactory result. It is important when stopping a plant that all shoots are dealt with at the same time. A balanced plant cannot result from pinching out being spread over several days. Not only will complete and balanced foliage cover be difficult to achieve, but flowering over the plant will be very irregular, some parts being in full bloom while others are merely in bud.

Right:
A plant which has developed suckers from the rootstock, with leaves and roots of their own

BUSH

The training required for a bush plant is almost identical to that needed for a shrub. However, it is vital that the plant can clearly be seen to be an individual, and that for exhibition purposes the first pair of branches emerge no higher than 38mm (1½in) above compost level. Suckering growths are not permitted, so when cuttings are taken it is important that any axillary buds that are likely to be buried in the compost are removed.

A shrub or bush-shaped plant

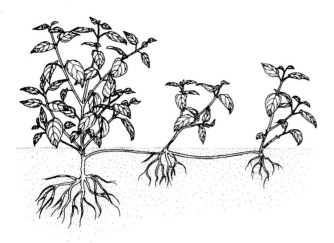

Below:
A very adaptable double-flowered fuchsia, Alison Reynolds, which can be trained into most types of growth. One for the showman as a bush or standard, it will be an almost certain winner in doubles classes once its cultivation has been mastered

BASKETS (FULL; WALL OR HALF)

Irrespective of when you decide to plant – either late autumn or spring – it is vital to start off with well-established plants of balanced growth. It is also essential that suitable cultivars are selected, for no form of training will turn an upright growing kind into a pendulous one. There are some excellent pendant fuchsias available (see page 132), as well as some cultivars of lax habit which can be successfully used for baskets with the assistance of weights.

When training plants for a show, consider the requirement of the schedule that baskets should be viewed from eye level. This is different for each of us, but most growers interpret this as the bottom of the basket being 1.8m (6ft) above the floor. Then, and only then, is the fuchsia observed at its most beautiful, perhaps just having to raise your eyes to receive the full benefit and beauty of a mass of hanging fuchsia blooms. Do bear this in mind when training your plants.

Unlike shrubs and bushes, basket fuchsias consist of more than one plant. It very much depends upon the vigour of the cultivar and the size of basket as to how many plants are required, but this can best be judged by looking at the baskets of successful exhibitors at fuchsia shows and making detailed notes. One golden rule, though, is to use a single cultivar in each basket. A mixture never works sufficiently well for exhibition, although on occasions it can present a charming picture for the domestic gardener when the various flower colours complement one another rather than clash. Remember too, that there are two basic divisions of basket fuchsias, those that produce flowers all over the plant and the ones that only blossom on the stem tips – and they rarely associate happily together.

One of the most important factors in producing an even, well-trained basket is the initial arrangement of plants. Most exhibitors will use six or seven plants for a standard basket. (Note that it must be the hemispherical wire type if it is to comply with British Fuchsia Society regulations for exhibiting.) Arrange

The British Fuchsia Society does not accept straight sided, flat bottomed baskets

Baskets must be hemispherical

the plants evenly around the edge of the basket, saving the largest individual for the centre. Most exhibitors will raise at least twice as many plants as they are going to require, so that they have an adequate choice at planting time. Usually all the outer plants are tilted slightly outwards, but this is not considered vital, for well-furnished plants should adequately fill and clothe the basket without resorting to this practice.

The central plant can be planted at the same time as those around the edge; however, many growers prefer to place an empty plant pot in the centre of the basket, so that an undisturbed place is reserved. The plant intended for the centre can then in the meantime be hastened along in a warm greenhouse. This plant is the key to the success of the basket and should be well furnished with growth, as it has to cover the centre and extend to the sides. Nothing looks worse than a basket without a bold centre. The aim should be to secure a domed or rounded top rather than a flat, uninteresting one. Growing the centre plant separately is the best way of achieving this, but you must anticipate its ultimate pot size as an empty pot of exactly the same size should be in the centre of the basket at initial planting time. Later, the centre plant can be placed in the hole created by the withdrawing of the empty pot. As basket fuchsias require copious quantities of water during warm sunny weather, it is prudent to make a depression in the compost around the central plant to allow for these large amounts of water.

Once successfully growing, basket fuchsias respond to the same kind of training routine as shrubs and bushes (see above). The growing points are pinched out at the second or third pairs of leaves, laterals allowed to develop and the process repeated until the basket is clothed with foliage. Sometimes branching does not cover the area intended, and it is then that adjustments have to be made. Do not permit the wood to harden before attempting to re-align a wayward shoot. While it is soft and supple, secure it either with a small wooden stake, a hairgrip, or large bent paper-

Below:
Preparing a
hanging basket
(a) Rest the basket in a
larger container
(b) Line the basket with
a 5cm (2in) layer of
damp sphagnum moss or
black polythene

(a)

(b)

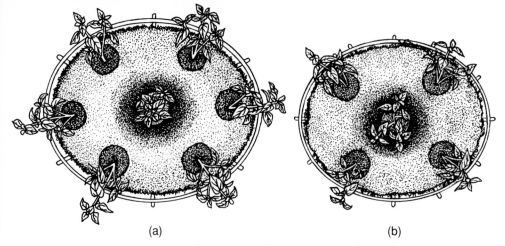

(a)   (b)

Above:
Planting up a hanging basket
(a) A 37.5cm (15in) diameter basket will require seven plants, from 9cm (3½in) pots
(b) A 30cm (12in) diameter basket will require five plants from 9cm (3½in) pots

Opposite:
What a delightful contrast of foliage and flower. Eva Boerg first appeared on the market over half a century ago – the picture shows clearly why it has stood the test of time. Best grown in trailing form

Right:
A half or wall basket. The British Fuchsia Society stipulates that half baskets must be demi-hemi-spherical. Plant one plant at the rear, and three around the front

clip. Peg the shoot to the surface of the compost or fasten it to the wire edge of the basket in the desired position, and allow the wood to ripen. The peg or wire can be removed once the branch has become set in position. Keep an eye on any aids to shaping, for if not removed soon enough they will cut into the stems. They must also be removed well before a plant is exhibited.

A half basket is exactly that: a basket which is treated in the same way as the full one, but with the intention of being viewed from the front and sides, so that all trailing plant material is pulled forward. The centre plant should be substantial and form the rear centrepiece of the display. In order to develop the correct shape and aspect, it is wise from the early days of training to have a substantial piece of board at the back of the basket, or to hang it on a wall. Good light is essential, and the front of the basket must receive the

best that can be offered if compact and even development is to take place.

Although hanging pots are a relatively new innovation and do not yet figure officially in the British Fuchsia Society's *Handbook of Judging Standards,* it is generally agreed that a hanging pot class is judged to the same standards as that of a hanging basket. The main requirements are that the pot is obscured by the foliage and the plant is well-balanced and well clothed with leaves and blossoms. In 1985 it was agreed that a choice of size of hanging pot would be placed on the British Fuchsia Society's master schedule for use by societies, giving the choice of including two classes in their schedule. One is for a 165mm (6 ½in) hanging pot in which an individual plant should be grown, with the other for a maximum pot size of 203mm (8in) in which one or more plants can be grown.

Selecting suitable candidates for training for hanging pots is as important as the training itself, for what is required is a naturally pendant cultivar which is amenable to the same pinching-out routine as recommended for the shrub and bush types. The scale of plant is also important, smaller-flowered cultivars like Harry Gray and Westminster Chimes being ideal. For the smaller hanging pots a single plant is desirable, even if you have no intention of showing and are not concerned about the rules. The same really applies to the larger pot. Although the skilful grower can successfully accommodate three or four plants in such a container, planting has to be carefully contrived in order to avoid the appearance of overcrowding, and a constant watch has to be maintained for the damaging and ever-present threat of botrytis (see Chapter 11).

STANDARDS (FULL, HALF, QUARTER OR TABLE)

When planning to grow any of the standard classes, bear in mind the ultimate size that you hope to attain and then choose a cultivar with a suitable habit and growth. Select a cultivar with large flowers and leaves for a large standard, and work down progressively to the smaller-flowered and foliage varieties for smaller, half and quarter standards. With modern cultivars it is possible to achieve the desired size much more quickly than previously. While hard and fast rules about which cultivar to grow for which finished plant cannot be given, watch out for Annabelle, Border Queen, Barbara, Flash, and Task Force. To get a clear idea of what will suit the particular purpose in mind look around at the standard entries at local shows and see which cultivars fill the bill. While a more rapid growth rate can be achieved by the careful selection of suitable cultivars, do not let this be the be all and end all of selection. Even with improved performance, showmen still like to take three years to finish a plant properly. The first year will hopefully produce the desired stem length, while the second and third years will be used to develop a balanced head.

As always, the foundations for a good plant are laid at the time cuttings are taken – not only the cultivar and material chosen, but also the period at which cuttings are taken. If heat can be provided, then cuttings can be taken early and the season of growth at the end of the year can be extended. This is the ideal situation, with early struck cuttings being able to continue growth, even if at only a slow rate, through their first winter. In reality the number of gardeners who are able to provide this facility is few, especially amongst the hobbyists, so cuttings must be taken during late spring if possible and certainly no later than early summer in the north.

The aim of the first year's growth is to produce as long and straight a stem as possible without any check in growth. At the same time, length must not be achieved by the plant becoming drawn, as will be the case in the autumn and winter if the warmth-to-light ratio is not very carefully maintained. An extension of the distance between leaf joints is an indication that the light and temperature are out of balance. There is too much warmth for the available light and the temperature must be reduced. The ideal is to achieve an even, short-jointed plant, but in reality this is easier said then done. For most growers, keeping the greenhouse temperature just above freezing at night will be the only way of coming close to this ideal.

Staking (see below) is very important from the outset. A good straight stem owes as much to the stake supporting it as to the speed of growth achieved. Not that training is the only consideration, for a standard fuchsia plant in full flower has a heavy head that demands support. It is vital that the stake gives support to the head as well as the stem. One of the commonest causes of weather damage with standard fuchsias used as dot plants in bedding schemes is the stake finishing at the top of the stem just beneath the head, as the head is then free to blow about. The stake should pass through the head and be cut off just beneath the domed top of the foliage. Always pay careful attention to the quality of the stake and the tie, especially when intending to exhibit. A perfectly grown plant can be ruined by an unpleasant-looking or inadequate stake and conspicuous ties.

The potting of standard fuchsias is also important, and it is here that the serious trainer can bend the rules. To grow a standard well it must have as unrestricted a root run as possible, so it is prudent to go an extra pot size up when repotting. When a plant is being trained it is essential that every effort is put into vegetative growth and the larger pot will help considerably, as long as the compost is never allowed to dry out. If the compost does dry out to the point where the plant shows signs of flagging there will be a check in growth, and instead of producing vegetative growth the plant will almost certainly come into flower.

The general management of a standard differs little from that of any other pot-grown fuchsia (see Chapters 3 and 4). The idea is to get the stem advancing as quickly as possible and to end up with as smooth a surface as possible. It is important that a stake is inserted from the outset and that as the plant grows the

sideshoots are removed. Do not remove the leaves at this stage as they are aiding the growth and development of the plant. There is no need to use a large stake yet: a green split cane is perfectly adequate. Insert this into the compost as close to the stem as possible, and as early as possible, without damaging the fragile roots of the young plant. Use soft green twine or tomato fillis to tie the stem in. Never use a coarse or unmalleable material for tying, as the stem is very soft and an indentation can easily be made. Once this has happened the damage is there for life, and can ruin an otherwise perfectly formed standard. Keep an eye on ties throughout the growing period and loosen them as necessary, for strangulation is a very real hazard.

As the plant comes close to reaching its desired height the lower leaves can be removed. Sometimes

Bealings has a white tube and sepals fading to pink, with an intense violet corolla. It is a double and is admirably suited to training as a quarter- or mini-standard; it will also make a good small bush. Very floriferous

during the growing period it may be apparent that if the leaves are left and removed later, then unsightly calluses and indentations will result when they are removed. This is a matter of personal judgement, for while the stem can remain clothed in foliage to the great benefit of the plant until the head is ready to be shaped, this must be weighed against likely lasting stem disfigurement. When the desired stem length has been reached, allow the next four pairs of axillary

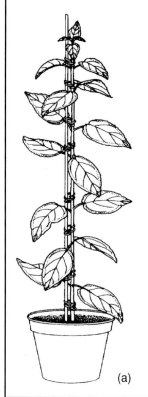

(a)

TRAINING A STANDARD

The first drawing (a) shows a young standard whip which has had all the side shoots pinched out. Decide what height you require for the stem length, then allow the next four pairs of side shoots to grow naturally, pinching them out as for a bush – remember that a standard is really a stem with a bush on top of it.

Make sure that the cane supporting the standard is at all times as tall or taller than the plant. As the drawing shows, plenty of ties should be used in order that the stem may be kept immaculately straight. However, do keep a check on them, making sure that they do not get too tight as this would strangle the stem.

The second drawing (b) shows the later stages of training, indicating consecutive stops. The most important feature in this example is the length of the supporting cane and the number of ties. Imagine what damage could be caused by moving this plant from one place to another, or by the wind blowing it about if it was being grown in the garden, perhaps even by the plant rocking about whilst being transported to a show – the large head would snap off at the point of the top tie. It is impossible to grow a straight stem with only two ties.

shoots to develop. The head can then start to be formed in the manner described for a bush or shrub (see above), for essentially a standard is a bush or shrub atop a long stem.

BALL

This is really another variation of the bush- or shrub-type plant (see above). The initial cultivation is the same, but when selecting cultivars you should look for

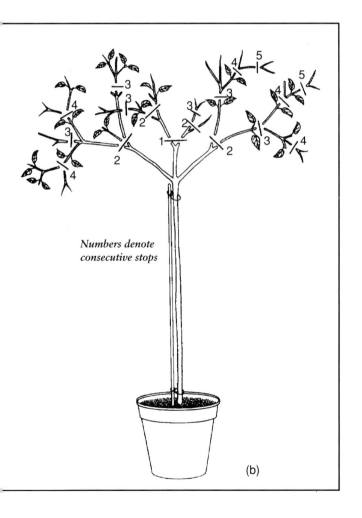

Numbers denote consecutive stops

(b)

A ball-shaped plant. A semi-trailing cultivar is grown, and is trained so that it hides the pot

those with upward-growing branches that then spread outwards, forming a sweeping habit but with pendant tips. Border Queen does this naturally and is ideal for training into a ball. Not that cultivar choice should be restricted to this mode of growth, for there are first-class kinds like Margaret Pilkington which do not exhibit this habit, yet can be trained perfectly by the careful use of weights.

The ideal young plant is short-jointed and is pinched out when it has produced two pairs of leaves. The overall aim of training is to keep the plant tightly pinched towards the centre to create density, at the same time allowing outer stems to grow unrestricted so that these can be used to hang downwards and obscure the pot. If the branches do not hang in the desired fashion, then weights can be used to pull them into place. Use weights sparingly and add them gradually, and never pull a branch down to the finished position all in one go. Attempt to arch the branches downwards and inwards towards the bottom of the pot.

Where the branches bend and curve new growth tends to break more freely from the leaf axils, and this helps in developing the desired dense habit. Once the initial framework is correct, the plant can be allowed to grow to the required size, the constant pinching back of lateral growths encouraging bushiness. This is one of the loveliest fuchsia shapes, but one of the most difficult to achieve, and it is therefore only rarely encountered at shows.

ESPALIERS AND FANS

This method of training is rarely undertaken in its traditional form, modern growers tending to train plants of this kind around a circle of wire, with a view to saving space. So it is sensible for us to consider this more popular practice first.

It is essential that a short-jointed cultivar like La Campanella is used to obtain the best effect. A well-rooted young plant is pinched out at the second pair of leaves. A circle of wire is then placed as close to the

plant as possible and, as the laterals grow, two are trained to go around the wire clockwise, and the other two anti-clockwise. As the plant grows it will produce sub-laterals, and these must be interwoven around the framework. Occasional pinching of these will help to ensure that the main branches continue growing. The principal shoots are not pinched until the opposite ones meet, some growers encouraging them to grow around the wire another time. In this way a nice thick framework is built up. Ambitious growers foresake the

Joan Pacey is an ideal cultivar to try as an espalier or fan. It is one of the larger-flowered single cultivars and will take plenty of direct sunlight

A ring-shaped fuchsia

regular circular arrangement and create shapes, perhaps a figure eight.

This is, of course, not strictly a fan or espalier, but is a development from that traditional system. True fans and espaliers are trained so that the flowers are viewed only from the front. However, the back should not be forgotten, for this must be well clothed with foliage to disguise the underlying framework. Both fans and espaliers grown for exhibition must have a short length of clear stem to indicate single plants, but this should be minimal. The whole plant of each type must be covered in both foliage and flower when viewed from the front, with an overall flat appearance. The whole should be symmetrical, with an even weight of branching and foliage throughout. Laterals should be symmetrically matched and of equal distance between one another. With these more than any other shape, it is important to have a pot that is visually of a suitable size and of such substance that the plant is not in danger of toppling over.

There are no restrictions or requirements of plant size, but most growers seek to develop a substantial structure. For a large specimen, it is vital to choose a quick-growing cultivar in order to produce a framework as quickly as possible. The production of a framework follows the same rules for each shape, it is just that the espalier has its laterals trained to grow horizontally to the main stem, while a fan has its laterals growing at an angle from the main stem. However, irrespective of the growth desired it is critical to the success of the plant to have a straight main stem, so it is prudent to insert a green split cane as close to the stem as possible immediately after the cutting has been potted. Later, when you feel that the pot size can successfully accommodate it, make a framework to support the entire plant. This can usually be made with canes, but whatever you decide to use ensure that it is neat, tidy, and not too conspicuous. The original centre support can then be removed.

Fuchsias do not conveniently produce their lateral

branches at the correct angle for the easy establishment of a structure. If the lower pair of axillary buds face along the line of the framework, and it is sensible to arrange the framework so that they do, the next pair will be facing outwards and to the rear respectively. Obviously these cannot be tied into the framework without considerable contortion, so they should be rubbed out between finger and thumb before they have an opportunity to sprout. If removed early enough they do not leave any unsightly, knobbly scars. The next pair of buds in the leaf axils above them will be facing in the desired direction.

Let the laterals grow to the full length required

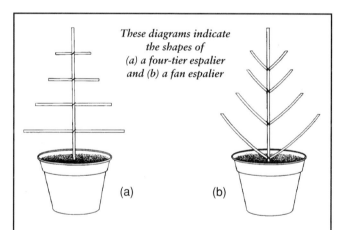

These diagrams indicate the shapes of (a) a four-tier espalier and (b) a fan espalier

(a) (b)

ESPALIER-TRAINED FUCHSIAS

When staking a four-tier espalier, ensure that the upright cane support does not exceed the plant height and that the lateral canes holding the branches are equal to, but not greater than, the length of the laterals themselves. The lateral branches should be tied to and on top of the lateral support canes, in order that plant growth will cover them and hide them from view. The size of plant you wish to grow will have a bearing on the size of supports needed. For example, if the bottom lateral should exceed three feet on either side of the stem support rod, then half-inch diameter supports would be required.

The fan type espalier is grown on identical lines to the tiered espalier, but for the fact that the laterals are trained to an angle of approximately 45°.

*A pot-grown espalier
trained over a framework*

before pinching out the growing points. Never pinch out the leading growth in order to promote sub-laterals. These will appear, albeit more slowly than if the branches had been stopped. Pinching out laterals will cause kinks and minor distortions to appear in their length, however neatly and regularly you tie them into the framework. Sub-laterals can be pinched back freely and tied in to provide the overall effect of a mass of foliage.

PILLAR (SINGLE-PLANT AND MULTIPLE-PLANT STRUCTURES)
Single- and multiple-plant structures have similar requirements. Let us consider the single-plant structure first. The technique is to take a well-rooted cutting of a suitable cultivar, like Border Queen, and pot it, together with a green split cane for support. The object is to train the leading growth to the full height desired, at the same time keeping it perfectly straight. The

whole stem should be as well branched as possible, the even development of laterals being encouraged all the time. Some growers lie the plants down for a period in an attempt to encourage even lateral development. An alternative is to use a single plant with two main stem growths, the aim being to try to produce a bush and standard growth on a single plant – not an easy task.

Perry Park: a strong-growing, single-flowered cultivar which is probably at its best when grown as a standard. It also makes a good bush or pyramid

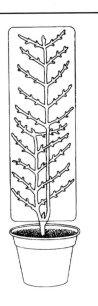

A TWIN-STEMMED, SINGLE-PLANT PILLAR

When growing a pillar in this way, the aim is to get the plant growing on two stems, one of which is stopped and treated as a bush (the bottom half) and the other is treated as a standard (the top half). Training in this fashion will give a uniform growth all the way up the plant, and will prevent tapering off at the top as in a pyramid. Grow the stems as close together as possible.

To achieve this, the plant must be pinched out above the second or third pair of leaves, rather than allowed to develop a strong main stem. All potential growths beneath the emerging axillary buds must be removed in order ultimately to prove that the plant is a single structure and, more importantly, to encourage the rapid growth of the two main laterals. Unlike a pyramid (see below), where the weaker growth would be removed, with a pillar both shoots are equally valuable and are afforded support. Use split canes and tie in the growth as close together as convenient, bearing in mind that one is going to be trained like a bush, the other as a standard. The ideal situation is where ultimately the two shoots can be merged to form what appears to be a single plant.

It is important from the outset to know exactly how tall you intend your pillar to be, for once the shoots have achieved half the pillar's ultimate height the growing point of one should be pinched out so that this can be trained into the bush section or bottom half. The other leader can be allowed to grow on and develop the head of a standard. Unlike the regular standard, when using this training technique for the formation of a pillar do not be in a hurry to rub out lateral shoots. It may be that some of the lower ones on the stem of the 'standard' will be needed to fill gaps in the 'bush' structure. Although removing laterals later will leave ugly scars on the stem, they are not noticeable in the same way as on a standard stem, for they are disguised by the burgeoning foliage around them. This training of a single-plant pillar results in what is usually referred to as a twin-stemmed, single-plant structure.

Multiple-plant pillars are grown in a similar fashion, but using three plants to a pot. Adopt a similar method to that used for multiple-plant pyramids (see below), but remember that the structure must be even in diameter from bottom to top. Pillars of this kind are difficult to grow well, but are very rewarding when they are a success. Both kinds take at least two years to develop a full structure.

PYRAMID (SINGLE-PLANT AND MULTIPLE-PLANT STRUCTURES)

The majority of fuchsia growers agree that this is one of the most difficult shapes to train. Getting evenness when viewed from all angles demands considerable skill. The shape, although roughly triangular, must draw into a sharp point at the top. To assist in getting the right shape, choose a short-jointed cultivar. Any that consistently produce laterals that are equidis-

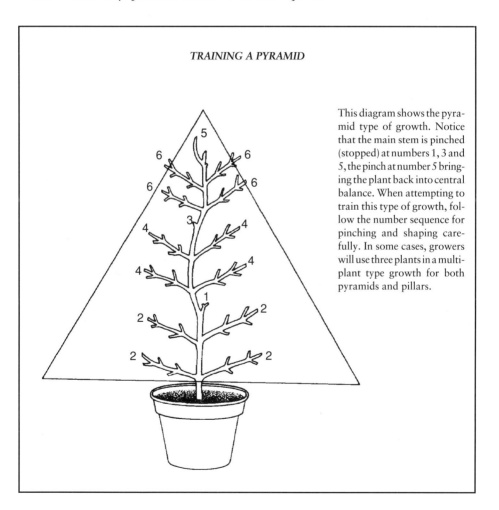

TRAINING A PYRAMID

This diagram shows the pyramid type of growth. Notice that the main stem is pinched (stopped) at numbers 1, 3 and 5, the pinch at number 5 bringing the plant back into central balance. When attempting to train this type of growth, follow the number sequence for pinching and shaping carefully. In some cases, growers will use three plants in a multiplant type growth for both pyramids and pillars.

tantly placed on the main stem should also receive consideration. A cultivar with a lanky or untidy mode of growth should never be considered for training into a pyramid, even though it may be free-flowering and have good-quality foliage.

The technique of shaping a pyramid is the same for both single-plant and multiple-plant structures. Use rooted cuttings that have been taken and rooted during early spring, to allow two long seasons of growth for completing the structure. The fewer interruptions in growth the plants receive, the more even the structure is likely to be. It is vital with pyramids, and also desirable with pillars and conicals (see below) too, that growth is strong and continuous. So, it is necessary to check regularly the condition of the rootball. Roots must not be allowed to run around the bottom of the pot until the final pot size is attained. If this happens during mid-growth, the plants start to set flower buds, which produces a check and impairs proper structural development. Regular watering, feeding, and ample light are all needed for unimpeded growth. As this is rapid, it is essential that staking is attended to regularly. Start with a split green cane right from the initial potting stage, and amend the support system as the plant grows. For show work, it is quite permissible to have a stake present, although this should be as unobtrusive as possible.

When starting a plant for a pyramid, remember that for show purposes a short length of clear stem must be in evidence to indicate single-plant structure. The same applies to multiple-plant structures – clear proof of the number of plants present is necessary. This is best achieved early on by rubbing out the lower two pairs of leaves as soon as the plant is considered to be of sufficient stature to be able to sustain the loss, generally when three or four pairs of leaves have been produced. Early removal prevents unsightly scars being produced on the stem. At the same time the leading growth is pinched out to encourage the production of laterals as close to the base as possible. Two laterals will be produced and it will be one of these which will become the new leader.

A week or so after the first pinching it will be obvious which of the two laterals is suited to becoming the leader. The stronger is always the one to select, and while it is still soft and supple it should be tied in to the split cane. Freshly produced laterals are always soft and delicate, so leave the inferior lateral intact until the new leader has been tied in, just in case this is accidentally snapped. Once the new leader is secured, the unwanted lateral is removed and the new leader is allowed to continue growing until 30cm (12in) or so high. It is then pinched out once again.

Although this is acknowledged as being the best system by all the top exhibitors, there is an alternative method of starting off a pyramid which some growers prefer. It follows along the same lines as previously described, but instead of pinching out and encouraging the development of laterals, followed by the selection of the stronger of these to take over as the leading growth, it allows the existing cutting to grow unrestricted to 30cm (12in). It is tied securely to a cane and then pinched out, as you would the new leader in the traditional training method. This method does, however, demand a degree of skill and experience to produce a good straight plant.

Irrespective of the training programme adopted in its formative life, the young pyramid requires stopping at 30cm (12in) in order to encourage the production of laterals. Every effort should be made to provide conditions conducive to the rapid growth of these, as they become the longest laterals and also the important basal part of the pyramid. A sparse, narrow base begets a shorter pyramid with a very narrow outline. To some extent the grower has to hope that the plant will behave rationally. That is, when a main stem is stopped energy will be diverted into laterals, and conversely when these are stopped it returns to the leading growth. This is all very well in theory, but in practice a main stem will often take off again before the laterals have achieved their desired length. In order to arrest this, affected plants can be laid on their side and turned regularly. This temporarily inhibits the growth of the leader and allows the laterals to continue extending. While this practice is quite common amongst exhibitors it can be a hazardous affair, and should only be used as a last resort unless you have considerable experience of its application.

Once the laterals have attained the desired length they must be stopped, thus encouraging the leading stem to grow away. Of course, it will once again be two laterals from the leaf axils at the point where the pinching out was done that will be vying with one another to become the new leader. This time you have no choice, for you must take that which comes from the opposite leaf axil from the original leader. If you ignore this recommendation, the plant will rapidly become unbalanced. The new leader should be carefully tied to its stake, which must always be taller than the growing plant. This process is repeated until the plant is of the desired height, pinching out occurring regularly at intervals of around 30cm (12in), but being more closely tied to the number of laterals breaking between each pinching out. If possible, these should be exactly equal in number each time. Most single-plant pyramids are considered to have attained their optimum height when the leading growth is 120cm (48in) tall. It takes two full growing seasons to develop a satisfactory structure for a show plant in this class.

Multiple-plant structures can be much greater in both girth and height. The training routine is identical, except that the leading growths of all three plants are tied together around a central stake.

CONICAL (SINGLE-PLANT AND MULTIPLE-PLANT STRUCTURES)

The training for conical fuchsias is exactly the same as for pyramids (see above), except that the overall shape must be that of a cone. It is important that a plant is in proportion to the pot in which it is growing. This is more difficult to achieve than when a wide-based pyramid is grown, for a plant with similar compost requirements can, in the case of a pyramid, be grown in a bigger diameter and more capacious pot than a conical and still be in proportion.

SMALL POT CULTURE

Small pot culture (see Chapter 6) depends for its success as much upon the selection of a suitable cultivar (see page 114) and the late taking of cuttings as it does upon training. Indeed, pinching out and tying in are exactly the same for small pot culture plants, as they are for those grown in a more traditional manner. Cuttings should be taken during late winter or early spring from cultivars that have suitably proportioned flowers and foliage. These should attain show standard by late summer.

GROWING FUCHSIAS FOR FOLIAGE EFFECT

This is a separate group of fuchsias for which there is sometimes a special class at a show. General cultivation is the same as for those grown for their blossoms. However, there are special considerations to bear in mind for getting the best out of them.

1. Always keep tightly potted, and use John Innes potting composts rather than soil-less brands.
2. Water sparingly and avoid getting water on the foliage.
3. Always grow the plants in the full sun to bring out the best colours, but avoid its scorching effects.
4. Plants placed outside during the summer always colour up best.
5. Keep off high-potash feeds and concentrate on high-nitrogen ones to help enhance the quality and colour of foliage.
6. Spray as little as possible with fungicides and insecticides. Use smokes whenever possible.
7. Under the new BFS rules, flowers are not taken into consideration when judging foliage classes.
8. Be patient. Remember that foliage cultivars take a lot longer to grow and come to maturity. Training is often more difficult too, for many have an unfortunate irregular growth habit. One of the best is Tom West.

6

Small Pot Culture and Bonsai

The small pot culture of the fuchsia has really taken off in the last decade. It must not, however, be confused with the bonsai type of growth.

SMALL POT CULTURE

It is of prime importance to choose small-flowered and small-leaved cultivars for growing and training into shape in 9cm (3½in) pots (see page 114). The new British Fuchsia Society *Judges and Exhibitors Handbook* has now changed its ruling on small pot culture. What used to be a plant grown in a maximum 12.5cm (5in) pot and with a length of bare stem from compost to under first branch joint of maximum 25cm (10in) has now become a mini-standard, and the small pot culture class is now comprised of pyramids, pillars, espaliers and fans. Baskets, which should really be termed hanging pots, are limited to a diameter of 15cm (6in), in which it is possible to grow two plants at most. Choosing cultivars such as Harry Gray or, even better, Frank Unsworth, will give a good display without the plant and the pot being out of proportion to each other.

The small pot culture class is a true test of the art of choosing and growing the correct cultivars, in order to produce a well-flowered plant with the correct size of bloom for the cultivar selected. The amount of top growth of leaf and flower must be in proportion to the size of the pot, but there are no hard and fast rules laid down in figures. Go to a fuchsia show, look at the

Opposite:
Frank Unsworth is a small, all-white, double-flowered cultivar. Short-jointed, and with a profusion of flowers, it is ideal for hanging pots and small pot culture

plants on view in these small pot classes, and ask the judge or a steward why a particular plant was selected as the winner. Eventually you will develop a rule of thumb to apply to the required size of a small pot grown cultivar, although, needless to say, everybody does not use the same yardstick by which to grow or judge plants. Experience is the best advocate of policy.

Very little has been written on the subject of fuchsias being grown as bonsai plants. By careful root pruning and keeping the general framework periodically pruned back, some very attractive little plants may be grown

FUCHSIAS AS BONSAI

This section on the bonsai fuchsia owes much to the work of Eileen Saunders in her *Wagtails Book of Fuchsias, Vol 3*. As she states, the fuchsia being a natural shrub, by growing it in pots it is to a certain degree already bonsaid. It only needs a little more regular pruning of the branches, the removal of more soil and the cutting back of more of the roots than normal, and a plant much smaller than usual can be achieved by trial and error (which is, after all, the basis of much amateur growing).

Flowering Bonsai

Displays of bonsai, grown in varying sizes and shapes of container, can be seen regularly at the larger flower shows, but how many of these are *flowering* plants? It is far harder to produce a flowering bonsai than a plant in a state of green leaf only – and yet the whole point of growing fuchsias is to enjoy their spectacular flowers! The key to growing a flowering bonsai fuchsia lies, in fact, in knowing that flowers are only produced on the current season's new branches. If these are left to flower on throughout the season the branching of new growth would outstrip the requisite limits of size for a bonsai type plant, so we need to shape the plant by pinching out and delaying flowering for a period. Many exhibitors will show a plant in the early July shows and then trim it back by an inch or two, thus removing all buds and flowers, to have it looking fresh and in bloom again for the late August and September shows. The smaller-flowered and -leaved plants are obviously a necessity to enable this type of training to be achieved.

Training

There are two possible ways in which to begin training a fuchsia as a bonsai: the first starts with a completely new cutting, while the second uses an already established plant which is then cut well back.

Cuttings Start with a newly-taken unrooted cutting, or with a cutting which has just formed a root system. Following the maxim of all good fuchsia growing – never overpot – it is critical that very small pots are used at this stage, and 2.5cm (1in) pots or 'thumbs' are a must. Small pots with meshed sides (often used by growers of alpines) are even better, as this enables root pruning to be attended to as soon as necessary.

Pruning The newly planted pots should be placed inside a larger pot filled with sand or grit. The reason for this is that by a quick twist of the pot, all the roots protruding from the pot side will be snapped off in the grit or sand, so keeping the rooting system within a tightly controlled area.

'Pot bound' is a widely used phrase, and is quite often misunderstood by the beginner. A plant's rooting system will grow downwards and out of the bottom of any pot if allowed to do so, and this is quite often the point at which the newcomer to growing in pots will make a very bad misjudgement. By tapping the plant

This pinky-peach single cultivar, Cambridge Louie, was all the rage with the showman when it first appeared in the list. It is still used by many as a mini- or quarter-standard, or as a 9cm (3½ in) small pot cultivar. A very adaptable plant

out of its pot, it will be seen that roots are covering the compost on the outside and the plant appears pot bound, but in fact the interior of the compost will not have a root in it. When a plant is completely pot bound the whole of the compost is an interwoven mass of roots, which feels quite solid when held in the hand and slight pressure applied. Experience is the deciding factor but the best guide, as with most flowering pot plants, is when the roots begin to emerge from the top of the potting compost – then the plant really is pot bound. To the beginner it would perhaps be more sensible to describe it as 'root bound'.

At the same time as the roots are growing, growth is also taking place above soil level in stems and leaves. As the roots are being kept well pruned (see above) so also must the green growth be kept well pinched by stopping the growth of the branches. Pinching out naturally stops upward growth for a while and all goodness is sent downwards to the rooting system, thus giving a boost to root growth. The two growths, root and foliar, are in fact interdependent, and one without the other means a dead plant.

The container Now that the plant has been kept root

A top show cultivar, Display is also suitable for training as a bonsai. In addition, it will make excellent growth and flower well as a hardy in the open garden, as shown here

pruned and the top growth pinched and pruned in proportion, the wood on the top growth will be beginning to harden and ripen, and it is time to think about moving the plant on into its final pot or container. Patience and time are needed to get to this stage: it will take many weeks, and perhaps months, of shaping and training to form the original cutting into the preliminary shape required for a bonsai.

From the moment that the cutting is selected as a future bonsai, the final container that it is to be planted into should have been considered, or even bought. The type of container is entirely up to the grower. Half pots and shallow saucers are ideal, but look also for the unusual items like tufa rock, tree branches in the form of small logs, or perhaps an interestingly shaped rock or stone.

Whatever you choose the 'container' will be shallow, and it is therefore very important that from stage one (ie planting the cutting) the very minimum depth of compost is used, as the eventual rootball of the plant will have to be shallow, and that any potting on stages must be more concerned with width than depth. The rooting system of a plant is basically divided into two parts: the roots at the bottom and well up into the compost are the ones which draw in the water, and those just below the surface of the compost are the roots from which plant food is taken up. An absolutely pot bound plant will be seen to have small roots just breaking the surface of the compost, as already explained. This is the state to which the plant should be grown in order that the small growth type of plant can achieve the ultimate in perfection.

In the same way that plants in the garden are mulched or, as in an alpine garden, a limestone chipping scree is used in order to retain moisture in periods of hot dry weather, a few small stones should be placed on top of the compost. Mulching is obviously impractical, as everything that has been done correctly towards training the bonsai is undone by, in effect, the addition of more compost. Retaining moisture is, however, vital in so small a container and everything possible must be done to ensure that the compost does not dry out.

Removal of Leaves Similar tasks are undertaken when growing and training a bonsai to those carried out when growing a normal-sized fuchsia in, say, a 12.5 or 15cm (5 or 6in) pot, but for slightly different reasons.

When training a normal-sized plant for show purposes, or perhaps just for use as a decorative greenhouse plant, it is very beneficial to nip out the larger leaves, particularly from the centre of the plant. The first reason for doing this is that it enables the new young shoots growing in and towards the plant centre to grow upwards and at their set angles of normal growth, thus enabling a naturally well-balanced and shapely plant to develop. This is important to the showman as when the large leaves are left in the plant centre, especially in the early stages of training, the new shoots will be growing in quite a bit of shade under the large leaves and they will become spindly and drawn. Equally important is the fact that the new young shoots are drawn upwards towards the nearest gap of light they can find, and will present a very unbalanced picture when they emerge into the daylight. Secondly, and perhaps more importantly, the removal of some of the larger leaves facilitates a much better circulation of air around and into the centre of the plant, thus reducing the chances of botrytis setting in which could mean the loss of a few branches in the middle of the plant or, more often than not, of the plant itself.

The benefits of improved air circulation around the centre of the plant are equally applicable to the removal of large leaves from a bonsai fuchsia. However, a fuchsia is quite a fast-growing plant as well, and when training a plant into bonsai form *all* the large leaves should be removed. (Once the plant begins to make growth in springtime there is always a continuity of young shoots, and this means a plentiful supply of green leaves). Plant food is converted by the process of photosynthesis, that is, through light being absorbed

into the leaves of the plant, so by removing the larger leaves the amount of food being converted will be reduced, thus slowing the growth of the plant – this is one of the arts of growing bonsai. Do, however, refrain from removing all the leaves in one fell swoop. It is much better to do it stage by stage: growing a fuchsia in this form is a great stress on the natural growth of the plant anyway, and patience is essential. In due course the leaves will be found to grow naturally smaller than normal.

Established Plants An alternative method to starting off with a cutting is to use an already well-grown and wood-hardened plant and cut it back very, very hard indeed. One of the joys of growing bonsai is that an irregularly shaped plant is a boon, because the last thing the grower is looking for is a perfectly shaped, show-type plant. Most important of all is the size and growth type of the cultivar selected, which should be small-flowered and small-leaved (see p114).

In spring plants begin to feel the urge to grow again after their long winter rest, and it is at this time that the plant or plants selected should be pruned back hard, branches and rooting system alike. Really prune back into the hard wood by cutting the old top growth well back, and spray daily until, as in growing the usual-sized fuchsia plant, the small green leaves of new growth appear. This is the sign that new root growth is beginning to take place below soil level, and now is the time to take the plant out of the pot, tease all the old compost out from among the roots and cut the roots well back.

Ideal for the 9cm (3½ in) class is this small-flowered cultivar, Shuna. A sport from Countess of Aberdeen, it is also a good cultivar to try for the bonsai type of growth

This method of using an old established plant as a starting point for bonsai has its drawbacks. Usually it will have been grown in a normal-sized pot, or be one that has been planted out annually into the garden as a bedder and then dug up and brought in for the winter. In either case, the rootball will be too large to cut back in one go to enable it to fit into a much smaller pot, and the top growth will also be oversized. It will therefore take quite a few sessions of pruning back before it can successfully be brought down to bonsai dimensions.

Compost

A bonsai fuchsia will remain in its final container for a number of years, and it is therefore essential to use the ideal compost from the word go. In fact, the compost mixes discussed earlier in this book (see Chapter 4) are quite adequate for use with bonsai, although they will be rather too coarse for use in a shallow container.

This problem is resolved by rubbing the compost through a 1.25cm (½in) sieve, saving the coarse material left behind for use in other planting projects. The resulting compost is then passed through a 0.5cm (¼in) sieve and the two gradings kept in separate heaps. That which passed through the sieve is then passed through another sieve of 0.08cm (1½²in) size, the dust collected being used for other purposes and the coarser compost saved in the top. There will then be two grades of compost remaining: the coarser one will be used in the bottom of the container, so allowing air to circulate in the compost, and the finer will be used as an upper layer to enable the fine feeding roots to penetrate it and get growing really well. As usual when potting a fuchsia, do not consolidate the compost too much but just tap the container a time or two on the bench, followed by some very light pressure using the thumb.

Feeding and Watering

The feeding programme will have to be rather different to that of a normal-sized plant. A high-nitrogen feed does not enter into the requirements of bonsai at all, and an advised feed would be one such as the Chempak No 10 with a content of 13% nitrogen, nil phosphate and 45% potash plus, of course, all the necessary trace elements. Start feeding when the tiny buds are just perceptible, using the feed at a quarter strength. Little and often is the best policy, but do make sure that the compost is slightly moist before feeding – feeding a plant which is dry at the roots will result in them becoming burnt by the feed.

There is no difference in the timing and method of watering a small plant to that used with a larger one. It is much better to water in the early morning, so that the moisture can be taken up during the hours of daylight. Also, if watering is done in the evenings the plant will sit in very wet compost throughout the night, which will do it no good at all. Nevertheless, a tiny plant will dry out very quickly on hot days due to the small amount of compost in which it is growing, and to allow it to dry out completely would be fatal. Foliar spraying is an ideal method of keeping the tiny plants moist enough to survive until the main watering is due.

Another reason for not watering plants in the evening is that quite a number of cultivars will be found to have brown marks on the underside of the sepals as the flower opens. This is because the plant has so much moisture in it that the flower buds sweat internally before opening, thus producing badly marked flowers. The rule therefore should be: main watering in the morning, and when spraying during the day do not do so in bright sunlight as this will scorch the leaves. Spray a plant that is in bloom very carefully, or again all the blooms will be badly damaged and turn a mushy brown.

General Care and Training
The shape of the finished product is entirely within the grower's control, but should of course be different from the normal bush shape. This is achieved through cutting back the hard wood and nipping out the very young shoot tips, and with practice and by learning from mistakes eventually the desired bonsai plant will be produced and enjoyed for many years.

Pests and diseases are exactly the same as for full-sized plants and treatment is identical (see Chapter 11). Overwintering the bonsai fuchsia is also identical to that already described in Chapter 4. It is entirely the grower's choice as to whether to keep the plant growing on in cool conditions throughout the winter period

Nellie Nuttall is an outstanding single cultivar for general use on the show bench. 12.5cm (5in) and 15cm (6in) pots of this beautiful red-and-white cultivar are sure winners and it is exceptional when grown in a 9cm (3½in) pot, but it is also an excellent cultivar to train as a bonsai

CHOICE OF VARIETIES

A suitable choice of varieties for bonsai type of growth could be:

Abbe Farges	Display	Nellie Nuttall
Beacon	Dollar Princess	Papoose
Beacon Rosa	Genii	Son of Thumb
Charming	Gracilis Variegata	Tom Thumb
Countess of Aberdeen	Lady Thumb	Westminster Chimes

This list contains a preponderance of hardy cultivars, which simply emphasises the basic requirement for plants which can stand up to the strains and stresses put on them to form bonsai type growth, yet still come out fighting to put on a bold show of flowers.

or to give it a rest before starting growth up again in the spring.

Producing a bonsai fuchsia really is quite straight-forward. Many fuchsia enthusiasts are growing mini-standards or plants in 9cm (3½in) pots with a great amount of success, and growing a bonsai is merely an extension of this which can be achieved with little extra trouble and effort, but which will provide a great deal of extra interest.

7

Propagation

The only reliable method of increasing named fuchsias is by stem cuttings. These are taken at various times according to the kind of plant envisaged, but for general home or garden decoration early spring and summer are the most popular periods.

Spring cuttings are taken from overwintered plants that are placed into warm light conditions and encouraged to sprout. In the case of bedding fuchsias, the old plants are usually discarded after the cuttings have rooted. Summer cuttings are taken from either outdoor or indoor fuchsias, the intention being to produce plants of sufficient size and quality to overwinter successfully.

The propagation technique used to produce plants for general decoration or show is similar; the only differences are minor and have already been noted in the previous chapter. Some forms of training require a cutting in which the basal axillary buds are removed, others demand that they remain intact.

SELECTING SUITABLE MATERIAL

Most parts of a fuchsia plant are capable of rooting if detached and pushed into a suitable medium, but to obtain the best plants careful selection must be made. Ideally cutting material should be vegetative, that is, not flowering and with no indication that it is likely to do so in the near future. Such a cutting will make a more satisfactory and malleable young plant than one taken from flowering material and, if it is of the current season's growth, it is likely to root more readily than any other. If it is impossible to find suitable non-flowering shoots, then flowering or recently flowered wood has to be used, all vestiges of flowering being removed during preparation. The ideal cutting is terminal material from a lateral or sub-lateral, although it is perfectly acceptable (and common practice) to root a terminal shoot if this is the result of a leading (main terminal) growth having been stopped. Strong plants are almost always produced from leading growths. Ideally, shoots selected for making cuttings should have developed sufficiently to allow them to remain turgid when cut, but should not have acquired the pinkish caste which indicates impending maturity. The latter kind of material is often hollow and virtually impossible to root successfully.

Having chosen suitable shoots, check to see whether any have their leaf axils in threes instead of pairs. Some cultivars, notably Snowcap, Celia Smedley and Anne H. Tripp, often throw out shoots with three axillary buds. This of course means potentially three basal shoots instead of two, so cuttings of this kind are ideal for plant structures that have a requirement for a strongly branching base. There is no guarantee that, once growing, the plant will continue to throw out laterals with groups of three leaves and buds, but a proportion will be like this and therefore careful pinching back can lead to a much bushier plant structure with no additional effort.

TAKING CUTTINGS

When suitable shoots are removed from the parent plant they should not leave a piece of stem that might die back to a leaf joint. The cuttings should be removed just above a leaf joint, so that the axillary buds that remain can break out unimpeded and form new laterals. The cutting material can then be prepared for insertion in the rooting medium.

A half-ripe cutting which has been prepared for inserting into the potting medium

INCREASING STOCK QUICKLY

Although it is ideal to take single cuttings with two or three leaf joints, if you wish to bulk up stock quickly there is a method of taking inter-nodal cuttings that produces satisfactory plants in bulk.

If you look at a vegetative shoot that is ready for propagating, it has three main parts: the soft, succulent tip, a length of more turgid stem and a ripening basal area. If the shoot is torn away with a heel – a piece of the old wood that remains attached – then this basal piece can be rooted and will make a satisfactory plant, providing that it retains one node or leaf joint and its accompany-ing axillary buds. It will take longer to produce roots than the better, softer material higher up the stem.

Moving further along the stem the material becomes more malleable and easier to root. Although cuttings do root better if taken at a node, it is nevertheless true that they root with relative ease anywhere along their stem. So we can use internodal cuttings – cuttings made be-tween the leaf joints. Providing each retains one node and its associated axillary buds, they should root without much effort.

If you are really desperate to increase your stock rapidly, then it is also possible to take internodal cuttings of reasonably turgid mate-rial and split it down the centre, thus retaining a single bud on each piece. These are a little more hazardous to root, but the occasional losses are nothing compared with the likely increase of stock.

Finally the very tip of the shoot can be rooted. The leaves have to be left more or less intact and may even rest on the rooting medium, so watch out for fungal diseases (see Chapter 11), especially botrytis.

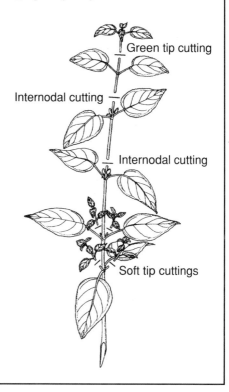

Green tip cutting

Internodal cutting

Internodal cutting

Soft tip cuttings

A detached cutting needs a balance between stem and foliage. Even after removing the lower leaves it is usually desirable to reduce the overall leaf area that remains, thereby cutting down on transpiration. The stem should be cut at a leaf joint to expose the maximum concentration of active cambium cells and thus enhance rooting. Hormone rooting powders and liquids are useful aids to propagation, as they encourage the initiation of root-forming cells and at the same time provide a degree of protection from fungal infections — once the end of the cutting has been dipped in the hormone preparation it can be inserted into the rooting medium. However, it is by no means essential to use a hormone rooting powder or liquid when propagating fuchsias, and many professional growers do not.

Gardeners have their own views about what constitutes the best rooting medium, but a mixture of equal parts by volume sedge peat and coarse sand, or peat and perlite (see Chapter 4) mixture, are satisfactory. Shallow pans are the most useful containers, the cuttings being inserted around the edge, just pushed into the compost. Nobody has discovered the reason why, but all cuttings seem to root better when inserted

Black Prince should be in every enthusiast's collection. A single red-and-purple, with the purple being very deep and often appearing nearly black. One of the excellent old ones

around the edge of a pan. Strangely, they appear to do better with neighbours rooting alongside them than in cells or pots of their own.

Modern fuchsia growers, however, are increasingly forsaking this method of propagation and, following the example of commerce, rooting cuttings directly into compressed peat pellets known as Jiffy 7's. Available to home gardeners for some time now, they are still treated with an unnecessary degree of caution by traditional growers, doubtless because of the pellets' bizarre appearance: small, flat, compressed discs. When placed in a seed tray and watered they quickly expand, filling a small, thin, netting container which serves as a pot. Consisting of high-quality, pure sphagnum peat with added nutrients, the pellets provide an ideal medium for both the rooting and growing on of cuttings. The netting eventually allows the roots of the plants to escape and penetrate the surrounding com-

This is Harlow Car, a very recent cultivar. It is a beautiful baby pink-and-white raised by Eric Johns, who lives close to the Northern Horticultural Society's gardens at Harlow Car

A coffee jar propagator. Cuttings are inserted round the edge of a small plant pot and the pot is then placed on the lid. The coffee jar is then screwed on and stood on a window ledge, but away from direct sunlight

Cuttings inserted into a plant pot and covered with a plastic dome, obtainable at any garden centre

post without disturbance, which is their great advantage.

Peat pellets effectively replace the old fashioned system of soil blocking (where blocks of compost were used without pots), and also the rooting of some cuttings directly into pots. Like soil blocks, though, pellets are very susceptible to drying out, which can cause severe checks in growth. It is also difficult to re-wet the pellets. Regular and careful watering is a vital component of this propagation technique.

Rooting takes place in three weeks, or thereabouts, and the young plants should be potted quickly into a good-quality potting compost in regular pots. Some gardeners express concern at the roots becoming entwined in the netting. For the most part this causes no problems, but it is wise to slit each side of the expanded pellet with a sharp knife before potting, taking care not to damage any emerging roots.

Weaning Rooted Cuttings

However cuttings are rooted, their chances can be much improved by being placed in a small propagator with a closed, humid atmosphere. They also need a reasonable temperature if they are going to root quickly. There is not an optimum, but they certainly require a minimum of 13°C (55°F) and no more than 21°C (70°F). Given a close atmosphere and warmth they root quickly, but by the same token they are unused to the outside world and require careful weaning. The

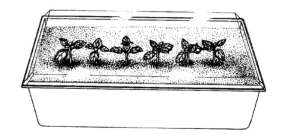

trick is to pot up the cuttings as soon as roots are initiated and to stand the young plants back in the propagator for a day or two. Once the shock to the developing root system has been overcome, the plants can be removed to the more hostile general atmosphere of the greenhouse. Most fuchsia cuttings readily accept the conditions under which we have to propagate them, it is just that better plants result more quickly if we can avoid a check in growth.

HYBRIDISATION

We hesitate to recommend that the fuchsia grower tries his hand at hybridisation, for it is generally acknowledged that there are enough, if not too many, cultivars available now. Some are so similar that it is questionable as to whether they should be named at all. Indeed, it is only in the area of hardy cultivars and amongst the triphyllas (see Chapter 9) that significant work can still be undertaken. But who are we to deny the fuchsia enthusiast the opportunity of attempting to come up with something different? However, if you do develop a hybridisation programme, you should discard almost all of the progeny. Only keep a plant for future development, or possible naming, if it really is different from everything that we have. If you come up with a winner then be sure to register it. This is the only way in which the current chaos amongst cultivars can be contained.

Before embarking upon a breeding programme, we perhaps ought to distinguish between hybrids and cultivar or variety hybrids. True hybrids are only made between distinct species of plants. Usually they are less fertile than their parents, sometimes being completely sterile, but often with floral parts that are larger and more persistent. Hybrid progeny are usually similar to one another, but often vary considerably from their parents. True hybrids can usually be crossed with a third species, the offspring being referred to as trispecific hybrids. The cultivar or variety hybrids are the result of a union between two cultivars or races of the

Above:
Cuttings inserted in a plant pot which has been covered with a clear plastic bag. The bag must not touch the cuttings, but should be supported by sticks or wire and then secured round the pot with a rubber band, so giving the cuttings their own warm, humid micro-climate

Left:
A cheap form of propagator is a plastic food tray – make some drainage holes in the bottom – covered with a clear plastic lid as used on food containers

THE FUCHSIA FLOWER

Before hybridising your fuchsias, it is important to know a little of their flower structure (see also Appendix 2). Each blossom is held on a pedicel or stalk. This varies in length from as little as 6.8mm (¼ in) to as much as 10cm (4in) depending upon species or cultivar. At the base of the flower is a quadricellular structure called the ovary which after fertilisation becomes the fruit. This contains ovules, which following fertilisation develop into seeds. Attached to the ovary, sometimes fused to it, sometimes separate from it, is the hypanthium or tube which itself extends to four sepals – the calyx. Tucked inside the sepals and joined to them is the corolla which consists of a varying number of petals. Protruding beyond the end of the petals and yet attached to the ovary is the style, with a receptive stigma at its tip. The length of the style is variable. Surrounding the style are eight stamens, the lower, stalk-like part being referred to as the filament, the upper, pollen-bearing portion the anther.

Pollination takes place when pollen grains from the anther are transferred to the stigma. The combination of a ripe pollen grain on a receptive stigma leads to the growth of a pollen tube inside the style down to the ovary. On reaching the ovary, the male nucleus fuses with a female nucleus and forms an embryo. Fertilisation has taken place. On occasions fancy cultivars that are hybridised give every indication that fruits are to be produced. They ripen, but contain few seeds or only shrunken ovules. This does not mean that the plant is sterile, more likely that the two are incompatible. This can sometimes be overcome by making the cross the other way.

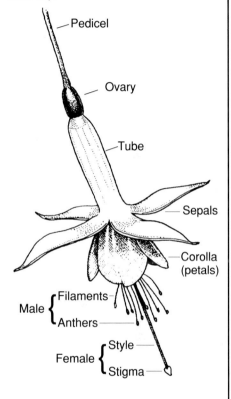

Left:
A beautiful, quality bloom, Pink Quartet derives its name from the fact that the corolla is made up of four little swirls of petals which give a quartered effect. It is ideal for use in the class for six blooms to be shown on a board

same species. They are usually vigorous, some obviously having the potential to be superior to their parents but, following the extensive breeding work of the past century and the number of cultivars produced, often this superiority is only in the eye of the breeder – so beware!

It is vital with all breeding programmes to maintain a record of crosses, indicating clearly the pollen-bearing (male) parent and the seed-bearing (female) parent. Dates of every operation from cross-fertilisation to the eventual flowering of the progeny should be carefully recorded. It may not appear to be of immediate value, but over the years a clear picture of the behaviour of various parents will be built up, often saving costly and time-wasting effort.

In conjunction with the recording system there must be a plan of campaign. This may have been instigated at the outset, for some breeders know exactly what they are looking for. Others discover interesting occurrences in their crosses and then develop a plan based upon that route. For either, it is useful to know which characteristics can be affected by hybridisation. Most are visual, such as vigour and stature, colour, earliness, shape and petal count of flower, quality and colour of foliage, but often more important are the unseen qualities of hardiness and disease resistance.

Amongst these characteristics it is also known that in fuchsias some are recessive and others dominant.

MAKING A CROSS

1   Select a suitable plant for producing the seed – this is the 'female' plant. Choose a flower that is in the bud stage. This is important as it may self pollinate before opening fully, or cross pollinate if allowed to open completely. Ideally the pollen should not be ripe enough to be shed.

2   Open the flower carefully and with a pair of fine, pointed scissors remove the stamens. Hold the stamens by the filaments so that there is no risk of squashing the anthers and liberating pollen. During this operation you must take care not to touch the style and stigma.

3   Enclose the flower and end of the shoot with a fine muslin or paper bag to exclude insects and prevent any chance of pollination. Do not use a polythene bag as this tends to accumulate harmful condensation.

4   Select a male donor plant and enclose several flowers that are approaching maturity in the same way, to prevent the chance of outside pollen contamination.

5   When the stigma of the female plant is glistening and appears to be somewhat sticky it is ready to receive pollen. Remove some stamens with ripe anthers from the plant that is to be the male donor. Lightly crush the anthers and then carefully apply the pollen to the female plant's stigma with a fine-bristled child's paintbrush.

6   The seed-bearing (female) plant must have the crossed flower protected by a bag until a fruit is seen to have set and begins to develop.

Note Sometimes in double-flowered cultivars the stamens on the seed-bearing plant become completely atrophied. It is often possible to correct this condition by starving the plant. This has the effect of reducing petal numbers and restoring the stamens to their correct state.

Recessive features are less evident, and easily masked by the stronger dominant characteristics. Light colours, for example, are recessive, dark colours dominant. Increased height is a dominant feature, dwarfness generally recessive. So, while it is relatively easy to breed a tall, dark-flowered fuchsia, it is extremely difficult to come up with a light-coloured, dwarf one. Add to this the fact that disease resistance and hardiness are variable factors, and you can readily appreciate the unpredictability of hybridising.

RAISING PLANTS FROM SEED

Seed raising is usually only undertaken following a breeding programme. It is not a satisfactory method of increasing your general collection, for most seedlings are inferior to named cultivars. It is true that species can be grown quite easily from seed, but unless they were flowered in isolation it is likely that mostly primitive, and probably inelegant hybrids will result. Only bagged blossoms, deliberately pollinated are likely to yield useful species seed.

The fruits of fuchsias are soft, rounded and generally deep maroon, violet or almost black when ripe. They are ready to harvest between late summer and early autumn. When ready for gathering they fall from the plant naturally, or as soon as touched. If you have a heated greenhouse the seed can be sown straight away. Not that seed requires a high temperature, it is just that young plants must be kept growing through the winter if they start life so late in the season. If you are in any doubt about your ability to maintain growth during winter, save the seed until spring. For the majority of gardeners this is the most sensible thing to do, labelling the fruits and keeping them in a cool, dry place. It is true that some viability is likely to be lost during storage, but this is more acceptable than running the risk of losing seedlings during the winter.

The seeds need extracting carefully from the pulpy fruits before sowing. It is important to remove them from the debris, for if any is sown with the seeds it is

All higher plants are dependent on pollination for seed production. Most of those with flowers are insect pollinated, but the fuchsia can be pollinated by birds – particularly humming birds, which do not have to perch on the flower to feed, so the blooms can be pendant. This is helpful in discouraging unwanted insects, and also protects the inside of the flower from rain

Red Spider, shown here on a patio wall, but equally good when displayed in a hanging pot or basket. A lovely, luminous red, self single

a potential source of fungal infection. Squash each fruit in turn between finger and thumb and wash off the contents in a saucer of water. Thoroughly disintegrate the fruit so that no seeds remain behind. When introduced to water, good fertile seed will sink, debris floats. It is thus a simple matter to separate them. Spread the seeds out on blotting paper to mop up surplus moisture and they are then ready to be sown.

This double cream-and-pink bloom is of Australian origin and is registered as the first yellow-flowered fuchsia! Needless to say, we are still waiting to see a yellow one . . .

Sowing the Seed

Fuchsia seeds must always be sown in trays or pans of good seed compost. Never be tempted to go out into the garden and scoop up ordinary soil for seed raising. Even though such soil may look quite reasonable, it is likely to be of too poor a structure for use in trays and pans. It will also almost invariably contain pathogens which will cause problems later.

Seed composts differ from potting composts in that they have few plant nutrients. The lack of fertiliser ensures that there is little likelihood of the tender seedlings being 'burned', and it helps to dissuade troublesome mosses and liverworts which frequently invade the surface of seed pans. Soil-based composts of the John Innes formula are ideal for raising fuchsias. Soil-less composts that consist of just peat, but with nutrients added, need handling carefully: you must be able to ensure a very smooth surface once the seed tray or pan is filled, and as the compost is so fibrous it creates air pockets in which the tiny seeds can become stranded.

The pans or trays that you use for seed raising should be filled with seed compost to within 1cm (½in) of the rim. A soil-based compost must be firmed down before sowing, but the peat types merely need putting in a pan or tray, filling this to the top and then tapping it gently on the potting bench. This, together with the first watering, will firm the compost sufficiently. Firming down soil-less composts only succeeds in driving out the air and making them hostile to root development. It is essential with *all* composts to firm the corners and edges with the fingers when filling a seed tray. This counteracts any sinking around the edges and prevents the seed from being washed into the sides, where it will germinate in a crowded mass. Seed compost can be watered from above prior to sowing. This is particularly useful with the soil-less types, as it settles the compost and allows any surface irregularities to be rectified before sowing.

Fuchsia seeds should be sprinkled thinly and then covered sparingly with compost, as they need darkness in order to germinate satisfactorily. Being fine seeds they are difficult to handle and distribute evenly, so mix them with a little dry silver sand. This serves as a carrier for the seed, and also shows where it has been sown. Once sown, only water from beneath. Stand the tray or pan in a bowl of water and allow the compost to dampen. Overhead watering can be disastrous, re-distributing the seed to the edge of the pan or tray.

Fuchsia seeds benefit from bottom heat, so if you have a soil-heating cable make full use of it. Warm compost promotes rapid germination and is particularly useful for gardeners who only have an unheated greenhouse. Where no heat is available, the addition of a sheet of newspaper over a seed tray or pan will act as insulation and create a warmer micro-climate. Although light can penetrate the paper, it is important to remove it as soon as the seeds have germinated. Light is vital so, as soon as the seedlings appear, place them where they can receive the maximum amount. This will ensure that they develop into stocky, short-jointed plants.

Fuchsia seedlings are very vulnerable to damping-off disease at this stage and watering should be carefully regulated. This unpleasant disease is prevalent in damp, warm conditions, invading the stem tissues of the seedlings at soil level and causing them to blacken, and the plant to collapse. Prevention is better than cure so, as a precaution, water all emerging seedlings with Cheshunt Compound (bought as a powder to be mixed in water).

Pricking Out

The seedlings should be 'pricked out' as soon as they are large enough to handle; that is, the crowded seedlings should be separated, lifted and spaced out at regular intervals in pans or seed trays. Ideally, seedlings should have their seed leaves fully expanded before transplanting, and the first true leaves should be showing. Fuchsia seedlings must be handled carefully, as they are very delicate and brittle. Never be tempted to hold a seedling by its root or stem as you can cause irreparable damage – always hold it by the edge of the seed leaf. Rough handling at the pricking out stage can lead to the spread of damping-off disease and the arrival of other pathogens.

The seedlings must be pricked out into a potting compost. As fuchsias are quick growing a standard soil-less potting mixture is adequate, although some gardeners prefer John Innes No 2 Potting Compost. Providing that there are no sharp temperature fluctuations and always plenty of light, the young plants should develop well. Apart from greenfly (easily controlled with a systemic insecticide, see Chapter 11), few problems are likely to be encountered until the plants are potted up individually.

8
Exhibiting

Fuchsias are essentially plants of the people, the majority of gardeners wishing to enjoy their exotic beauty in house, greenhouse or garden. However, there is a body of enthusiasts who have an inborn competitiveness, and it is for these showmen and those who aspire to join their ranks that this chapter is written. Showing fuchsias encourages excellence in cultivation, which is no bad thing, and much of what is written here can help to improve fuchsias in home and garden as well.

FINDING OUT ABOUT SHOWING
Before entering into the show world it is important to find out at first hand what is involved, not just in the cultivation of the plants, but also the results that are expected. An indication of the standards to be reached can be more quickly and readily appreciated by a visit to a specialist show.

To find out exactly what a judge looks for, volunteer to be a steward on show day. It is a great opportunity to learn. Many stewards ask judges if they will give reasons for their decisions, and in a close finish for an award it may be just a small factor like a dirty pot or label that will tip the balance. The top of the pot may be covered with moss or algae, or perhaps have one or two lingering dead leaves or flowers on it – presentation is so very important. All such points will be freely imparted by most judges, giving a real insight into the

Opposite:
This is the brilliant red-and-white double, White Lace. A good, bushy hardy and show plant. Very adaptable

show world.

The annual show is the shop window of any local fuchsia society. Lecturers have encouraged members to improve their techniques during the winter months, and show day is when their advice is put to the test. It is tremendous fun being involved with the annual show, especially as an exhibitor. Even when the greenhouse looks full of plants that are too far gone or not

---

THE BEST CULTIVARS FOR THE SHOW BENCH

Shrub or Bush

Alison Reynolds	Celia Smedley	Jean Clark
Annabel	Cloverdale Pearl	Margaret Roe
Ann H. Tripp	Crosby Soroptomist	Meike Meursing
Atlantic Star	Dollar Princess	Nellie Nuttall
Beacon	Doreen Redfern	Patio Princess
Beacon Rosa	Dusky Beauty	Pink Fantasia
Border Queen	Eden Lady	Shelford
Brenda White	Halsall Beauty	Superstar
Cambridge Louie	Icecap	Waveney Waltz
		Westminster Chimes

Hanging Basket

Border Queen	Eva Boerg	Marinka
Cascade	Harry Gray	Natasha Sinton
Derby Imp	Jack Shahan	

Hanging Pot

Anna of Longleat	Harry Gray	Waveney Gem
Auntie Jinks	Lindisfarne	Westminster Chimes
Derby Imp	Natasha Sinton	

Standards

Annabelle	Celia Smedley	Perry Park
Barbara	Flash	Task Force
Border Queen		

9cm (3½in) Pots

Bealings	Little Beauty	Nellie Nuttall
Dusky Beauty	Love's Reward	Superstar
Jean Clark	Minirose	Westminster Chimes

---

quite ready, take a chance and exhibit – it is much more satisfying being a participant than a spectator. If your plants are not ready on the day, those of many fellow members are likely to be similarly placed. So, in fact, any well-grown plant should have a chance of a card. Remember, too, that a plant always looks better when properly staged on a show bench than when growing in the greenhouse.

Espaliers and Fans

| Border Queen | Micky Goult | Prosperity |
| Joy Patmore | Phyllis | String of Pearls |

Pyramids, Pillars and Conicals

Barbara	Mission Bells	Snowcap
Border Queen	Pink Pearl	Tennessee Waltz
Celia Smedley		

Small Pot Culture

Bealings	Heidi Ann	Nellie Nuttall
Derby Imp	Lady Thumb	Son of Thumb
Estelle Marie	Linda Goulding	Tom Thumb

Species and Species Types

F. arborescens	F. fulgens	F. splendens
F. denticulata	F. hemsleyana	Ariel
F. encliandra	F. procumbens	Speciosa

Triphylla Cultivars

Andenken an Heinrich Henkel	Korralle
Billy Green	Mary
Gartenmeister Bondstedt	Thalia

Ornamental Foliage

Autumnale	F. magellanica var. gracilis variegata	
Cloth of Gold	Pop Whitlock	Sunray
		Tom West

Hardy Cultivars

Beacon	Genii	Papoose
Charming	Lady Thumb	Tom Thumb
Dollar Princess		

133

PREPARING FOR SHOWING

The preparation of show plants really starts at the time the cuttings are taken. Success not only depends upon taking the cuttings from good, healthy, vigorous material, but also upon the cultivars from which they are selected. It is accepted by seasoned showmen that there are a relatively small number of cultivars that make good show specimens, and a visit to any show will reveal the best ones to pick for exhibiting.

With the careful selection of plant material and ordered cultivation, even the novice fuchsia grower has an opportunity of winning an award. The greatest handicap to success is the attitude that, being a novice, there is little opportunity of knocking seasoned showpeople from their lofty perches and therefore it is not really worth entering. Self assurance is as important an asset in a fuchsia showperson as is the knowledge of the correct method of feeding plants for exhibition.

Not that there is much to know about feeding other than that already described. If your plants are running a little behind schedule and need a final push to reach perfection for show day, they can be given a boost by adding saltpetre when watering. Saltpetre is nitrate of potash and should be added to the water at a rate of 1g per 9.5 litres (½oz per gallon). A single application ten days before a show will give the blossoms a boost, hastening their development and improving their colour.

It is advisable to check the plants well ahead of a show for signs of pests and diseases. A regular spraying routine must be continued throughout the entire growing period if foliage and flowers are not to be distorted or disfigured. However carefully this is followed though an odd greenfly can slip through, or changing weather can provide perfect conditions for the rapid development of mildew, so it is imperative that the plants are checked regularly before exhibiting and pest control measures taken whenever necessary. Apart from being acutely embarrassing for the exhibitor, it is unfair to

Dark Eyes. This red-and-violet-blue double is one of Allan's favourite double cultivars. Easy to grow, and one for the show doubles classes

show infested plants alongside the clean, healthy specimens of other entrants.

There can be unforeseen last-minute problems in even the best-ordered greenhouse. However, much can be done to overcome them by rehearsing the preparation and removal of plants for a show a few days beforehand. It would not be the first time that an exhibitor with a potential prize-winning plant discovered that it was so large that it would not pass through the greenhouse door! Look at transport arrangements too – be prepared.

Checking the Schedule

Before coming to a final decision about the individuals to be shown, it is important to check the schedule. Read it carefully and thoroughly, as there is nothing more disheartening than exhibiting a beautifully grown plant that receives an NAS (Not As Schedule) ticket. The plant and pot must conform to the schedule in every respect.

Make sure that single-flowered cultivars have only four petals. Semi-doubles should have five to seven petals and, under the new rules, must be shown in the singles class. Any plants with eight or more petals should be entered in the doubles class. Do not rely upon the cultivar's description in a book or nursery's catalogue to determine whether it is a single, semi-double or double – the decision as to which class an individual should be entered in must be based upon the characteristics of the plant in the greenhouse. One of the biggest offenders is Meike Meursing. Nobody seems sure what to exhibit it as. Ann H. Tripp, Brutus and Lord Roberts are other popular examples. When faced with this dilemma, enter the plant in the 'any cultivar' or multipot class. Make sure that the schedule of your society's show includes such classes. There is no reason why a society should not provide a class specification for every plant, and when the show committee provides this breadth of opportunity it is important to see that all classes are well supported.

What the Judge will be Looking For

A judge will usually walk around all the plants in the hall before judging individual classes. She or he will cast a glance at every plant in each class. More often than not the winner will be fairly obvious: the problem is usually sorting out the second and third. What is it in a winner which catches the judge's eye in the first place? Invariably it is quality of growth. The size and balance, quality of flower and foliage, and general wellbeing of the plant all show a high degree of skill in cultivation – what the British Fuchsia Society describes as 'cultural excellence'.

When it comes to dealing with individual plants, the judge will be seeking all the good points and marking them. She or he will only look for faults when the decision is very close and something has to be found to separate plants. Therefore dirty pots, dirty saucers, dirty labels, absence of a label, tidiness in staking and tying, when this is necessary, are all points to consider carefully when staging an exhibit. The flowers must be typical of the size, form and colour appropriate to the cultivar and they must be fresh and clean. The degree of difficulty in growing a specific cultivar will also be taken into account by a good judge. For example, a white-flowered cultivar like Ann H. Tripp or the pale-flowered Flirtation Waltz is always much more difficult to get to a show without bruising and browning than its darker-coloured cousins.

Dressing a show plant is very important. It makes all the difference to the presentation of the plant to the judge. Lift out gently all blossoms that are hidden in the foliage: it is amazing how many flowers can be discovered lurking amongst the leaves. Use a pencil rather than fingers to tease them out, as they bruise very easily. Never succumb to the temptation of popping nearly open buds. A good judge will spot it, and when it is done on many buds the overall appearance of the plant is spoilt. It is preferable to see good, well-formed, normal buds rather than forced-open flowers. Ideally, a show plant should be well flowered all over with no blank spaces, and there should also be complete foliage cover. All discoloured leaves must be taken off before staging time, as should all the blooms which are past their best. With hybrids, take off seedpods or berries when these are in evidence. However, with species and those popularly referred to as species types (see Chapter 9) these should remain, as they add to the plants' decorative quality.

A colourful display of flowers exhibited by the West Yorkshire Fuchsia Society, which won its class at the Great Autumn Show at Harrogate

It is vital that all pots are clean. Show rules stipulate that a plant must be shown in the same size and kind of container in which it was grown. There is nothing improper in providing a new, clean pot of the same size on show day, and it helps to set the plant off beautifully. Ensure that the soil surface is clean and free from plant debris and green moss or algae. Plants must be in proportion to the size of the pot in which they are growing – often excellent plants fail because the pot or plant is of disproportionate size. Use stakes or tying wires only when absolutely necessary. British Fuchsia Society rules state that staking should be at a minimum and unobtrusive. This is generally interpreted as one or two stakes for bush or shrub plants and a single stake or cane for a standard. Never use ribbon or plain string: green garden twine is much more acceptable.

A judge will pick up every plant to see what is at the back and hidden from view. Most growers acknowledge that every plant has a bad side: it is up to the judge

---

A GUIDE TO DRESSING

1. Make sure that all plants are free from pests and diseases.
2. Remove all spotted, yellow or discoloured leaves.
3. Remove any marked or faded blossoms.
4. Remove seed pods or berries, except on species and those referred to as species types.
5. Make sure that pots are clean and not cracked, chipped or split (use new pots).
6. Scrape stale compost and debris from the pot surface. Replace with fresh compost.
7. Adjust any branches that are out of place. Tie them in discreetly with green twine and stake carefully if necessary.
8. Lift out any blooms and buds that are hidden by the foliage.
9. Water well on the morning of the show, wetting only the compost, never the flowers or foliage
10. Provide a new, clear, well-written label.

to recognise it. When a plant has been prepared, stand back and take a good look at it. The judge will certainly do this and can almost be guaranteed to notice anything that is amiss. Once judging has started it is too late to make any changes, and the judge must disqualify any misplaced or irregular exhibits. Until recently, he would have looked for extra sepals on cultivars like Snowcap, Pacquesa and Phyllis, but these are now accepted under BFS rules (in our opinion a backward step), and for extra petaloids (see Appendix 2) on cultivars such as Meike Meursing, Ann H. Tripp and Lady Thumb.

GETTING THE PLANTS TO THE SHOW

One of the biggest headaches for an exhibitor is getting his or her plants to the show undamaged. By and large it is as difficult, and requires as much effort, to pack and transport plants successfully to a local show as it does to one a half day's journey away. Tight packing is the key to success, together with the liberal use of pieces of old net curtaining. This, put around the heads of bushes, shrubs or standards, prevents the branches moving and becoming damaged or broken. It also prevents the blossoms from dancing about and bruising badly. This is especially vital for white or pastel-coloured cultivars.

Putting the curtaining on the plants is a tricky job which needs two people. Turn each plant upside down and tie the curtaining as close as possible around the base of the main stem next to the lower branches. Draw the curtaining carefully over the head of the plant, gently pulling it as tight as possible without damaging the branches, and then tie it again above the head. It is also possible to pack plants close together in cardboard boxes when only a short journey is to be made, or to make special pot holders that will hold the plants upright. Sometimes it is necessary to provide temporary stakes to give added support. Remove them all when staging, for only a limited amount of staking is allowed (see above).

A fuchsia draped in net curtaining, ready to transport to a show

STAGING THE EXHIBIT

By the time that plants have safely arrived at a show, all the pre-checks regarding their eligibility under the schedule, together with the appropriate manicuring, should have been completed. It is important to arrive in plenty of time to make a good and unhurried job of staging. Collect entry cards from the show secretary and stage the plants in the appropriate sections. If a competitor's plant is interfering with your space ask a steward to move it. Never touch anyone else's plant. If it is your first effort at staging and you are unsure about some aspect, ask another exhibitor: they are almost always willing to advise. So are judges. If a prize card is not forthcoming ask the judges where you went wrong – they are usually happy to tell you.

A GUIDE TO STAGING

1   Check that entries are correct: single-flowered plants in single classes, semi-double in single or multi-pot classes, double-flowered plants in double classes.

2   Check that labelling is complete and correct.

3   Tease out any leaves or blossoms that have become misplaced on the journey.

4   Remove any fading leaves and blossoms.

5   Move each plant around until its best side is facing the judges.

6   In classes for multipot entries, raise the rear plants up slightly by placing an upturned saucer under them. Never balance plants upon an upturned plant pot; this is too precarious.

7   When an odd plant in multipot entries is smaller than the rest, place it at the front of the exhibit. Those behind do not then require raising at all.

8   Do not water plants before judging takes place. It does not endear the judge to your exhibit if she or he gets soaked when examining a plant, and if you use a saucer this often sticks to the pot and can cause damage when it drops off, as well as splashing water everywhere to the general detriment of the exhibit. (When the show is longer than a single day, saucers are usually placed beneath each plant by a member of the show committee to permit watering.)

9   When you think that you have finished staging your exhibits, look around at the competition. Will your plants compete satisfactorily? If not, is there anything else that you can do by way of presentation to ensure that they do?

JUDGING

The British Fuchsia Society lays down rules, regulations and standards for showing, which are reproduced below.

Stewards

As the Show Schedule is the basis on which the Show is judged, the Steward must be familiar with its Terms and Rules so that he can advise exhibitors or draw their attention to any exhibits not conforming to the Schedule.

The Steward should be present some time before judging commences so as to familiarise himself with the layout of the Show and the starting and finishing point of each Class. He should ensure that each entry is correctly staged, pot sizes and stem lengths are correct as per the Schedule, and that the relevant Exhibitors Card is placed face downwards in front of each entry.

The Steward should be there to meet the Judge on his arrival at the Show and should during judging be ready to check pot sizes and stem lengths if the Judge requires confirmation. He should indicate to the Judge the start and finish of each Class and the number of entries therein. He should not converse with the Judge during judging, but be ready to answer questions or clarify points if required.

As exhibits winning prizes may have to be reconsidered for further awards, Prize Cards and the relevant Exhibitors Cards should, for the time being, remain face downwards.

The Steward should check the progress of judging through the Schedule and ensure that all Classes are judged. When judging of the Classes has been completed the Steward should ensure that all Special Awards are made and be able to indicate to the judge which exhibits are eligible for these.

The Steward should be completely impartial, and it is recommended that a Steward should have had previous experience of exhibiting at a Fuchsia Show.

Judging Procedure

All Judges must be fully conversant with the Show Schedule.

An experienced Judge is not expected to be required to use score cards on his or her rounds of judging, but may do so if he or she finds it helpful to do so, in which case points are awarded as follows:

One of the newer cultivars, Robbie is well covered with pink-and-white blooms – when fully open the flowers resemble flying saucers

Quality and Quantity of Bloom 6
Quality and Quantity of Foliage 6
Cultural Proficiency   6
Presentation   2

Total   20

The BFS recommend that no Judge however experienced should be asked or required to judge any class on his or her own.

It is usual that Judges look over the entire class or section involved to determine the overall quality of the group, which will also give a guide to the overall rating of the exhibits.

This done, the manifestly inferior entries will be eliminated for lack of cultural competence or non-conformity to the Schedule etc, and the remaining entries are then subjected to a more detailed scrutiny. Evaluation will continue until the final decision is made. Judges should remove plants in contention for closer inspection and every endeavour to replace them as found will be made. Plants marked NAS (Not As Schedule) must always be followed by a note giving the reason, and such plants will not be eligible for a prize, cup, trophy, or other type of award at that Show.

It is acknowledged that personal preferences and prejudices are held by some Judges. The Judge should recognise this fact and be particularly careful not to be swayed by essentially personal views.

Absolute fairness and a complete lack of bias are the essential obligations of good judging.

Definitions

Bush A plant which may be grown on a single stem not exceeding 1½in (38mm) in length or on shoots produced from below soil level. The entire plant should be covered with an abundance of foliage and flower, according to the cultivar or species, presenting a balanced symmetrical plant when viewed from all angles. The plant should be in proportion to the size of the container. Stakes and ties if used should be unobtrusive.

A Basket (Full) This type if growth is one in which an optional number of plants are grown in a hemispherical wire or plastic basket to be viewed from the top and sides when displayed in an elevated position.

The plant growth must fill the centre and top of the basket and continue to surge over the edge in a sweeping cascade. Uniform growth, clean foliage and an abundance of flower, according to the cultivar or species, must continue to at least the depth of the container and should be evenly distributed from the crown to the end of the trailing growths. Ideally the container should not be visible when viewed from eye level. The size of the basket must not exceed that stated in the Schedule.

A Basket (Half or Wall Basket) This type of growth is similar in many ways to that of a full basket except that it is demi-hemi-spherical and designed to hang on, or be attached to, a wall and is viewed from the top, front and sides.

The number of plants is optional and should cover the entire crown, surging over the front and sides of the container to present a fully balanced, evenly distributed display of abundant foliage and flower, according to the cultivar or species, covering the crown to the end of the trailing branches. Ideally the container should not be visible and its size should not exceed that stated in the Schedule.

Hanging Pot This type of growth is similar to that of Baskets and Half Baskets and cultural proficiency is assessed in the same way. One or more plants may be used.

Standard (Full) The length of stem clear of all growth from soil level to the first laterals shall be not less than 30in (762mm) nor exceed 42in (1067mm).

The stem shall be straight, free of knots or other ugly blemishes and may be supported by a single stake. The whole head should be a profusion of branches, presenting a full and balanced effect of lush foliage and flower, according to the cultivar or species. The head of the plant and the stem should be in proportion to one another and the whole of the plant in proportion to the container.

Standard (Half) The length of stem clear of all growth from soil level to the first branch should be not less than 18in (457mm) nor exceed 30in (762mm).

Cultural details are as for a full standard.

Dusky Beauty is a delightful single and ideal for the 9cm (3½ in) pot class. Floriferous and short-jointed, it is a winner wherever shown

Standard (Quarter) The length of stem clear of all growth from soil level to the first branch should be not less than 10in (254mm) nor exceed 18in (457mm). The head should be of good overall balance. Cultural details etc are as for a full standard.

Mini-Standard The length of stem clear of all growth from soil level to the first branch should be not less than 6in (152mm) nor exceed 10in (254mm). The maximum pot size permitted is one of 5¼in (133mm) in diameter.

Cultural details etc are as for a full standard.

Espalier and Fan Espaliers and Fans are plants trained on a latticed structure. The laterals should be matched symmetrically on both sides of the plant centre. Espaliers should have horizontally trained laterals and Fans should have laterals trained into a fan design. All laterals should be fully covered with foliage and flower according to the cultivar or species, and viewed from the front. Although viewed for frontal effect, the rear of the latticed structure should be well covered with good clean foliage. The height of the plant must be in good proportion to the width.

Pillar A plant growth developed to produce a uniformly cylindrical structure fully covered with foliage and flowers.

The relation of height to diameter, and constancy of diameter from bottom to top of plant(s) should produce, when viewed from all sides, a graceful column or pillar of abundant foliage and flower, according to the cultivar or species. The overall size is unrestricted. A single central stake is allowed.

Pyramid A plant growth developed to produce a uniformly tapering structure from bottom to top. The pyramid shape must be maintained when viewed from all sides. The overall effect should be that of a tall tapering tree fully covered with foliage and flower. A single central stake is allowed. Overall size is unrestricted but good balance is expected.

Small Pot Culture A number of fuchsia species and cultivars are eminently suitable for this type of culture and these are normally found among the smaller flowered types.

Maximum pot sizes will be limited to those listed below. Smaller growth examples should be proportionate to the size of their pots.

True proportions of plant form will be expected. Good foliage and flowers, typical in size, form and colour for the plant exhibited.

Pyramids, Pillars, Espaliers and Fans will be allowed a maximum pot size of 5¼in (133mm) diameter.

Baskets will be a maximum of 6in (153mm) diameter.

THE SIX FLOWERS CLASS

The class for six flowers attracts a great deal of attention from judges, exhibitors, and viewing public alike. It is always one of the most difficult to judge.

The boxes which are provided by the society holding the show are made of thin plywood with dimensions approximately 8in x 6in x 2in and are painted black. Six holes are drilled in the top equidistantly and into these holes is pushed some plastic tubing, in length just a fraction less than the depth of the box. The lower end is then sealed up with putty, waterproof tape or whatever. This enables the tube to be filled with water in order that the flower can survive when placed in it. A warning here is not to overfill the tube, as quite often when the flower stalk is pushed into a full tube the excess water will make a pool on the box surface. The flower will then have to sit in it, with the result that it will be damaged and stained brown. Keep the box dry and always carry a few spare flowers with you.

The blooms should be as near perfect as possible, clean and free from all blemishes. The perfect flower should be fully open, the faintest touch of pollen may just be seen and the pistil must be at the vertical and not hanging limp. A bloom full of pollen with a dark coloured stigma is way past its best. Most shows only ask for a box of six flowers, named if possible, but we like to see a class of six blooms of the same cultivar. It is a real challenge to get six all identical, and only the grower with a large number of plants will be able to find enough blooms to do it. Therefore, most shows go for any six flowers, so giving the grower with only a few plants an equal chance of gaining success.

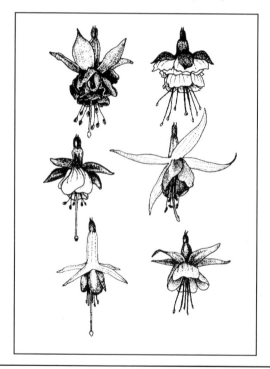

Affiliated Societies Display The prime consideration of this entry will be attractiveness of arrangement, design, colour harmonies and contrasts. Plants should be of good quality with fresh flowers and clean healthy foliage in the total overall display. Structural paraphernalia, pots etc, should be restricted from view.

Species These should be grown freely or with the minimum amount of training necessary to promote branching. Decorative fruit should be allowed to develop as an added attraction. Clean foliage and fresh flowers and/or fruit are expected. Stakes or other training media may be used but should be unobtrusive.

Species Hybrids and Variants (Excluding Encliandra) These should be grown freely or with the minimum amount of training necessary to promote branching. Decorative fruit should be allowed to develop as an added attraction. Clean foliage, fresh flowers and/or fruit are expected. Stakes or other training media may be used but should be unobtrusive.

Encliandra Section *(Breviflorae)* Species and hybrids may be exhibited in these classes. Cultural proficiency will be assessed on an abundance of healthy growth, overall freshness and high quality of foliage and flower. The decorative fruit should be left on the plant. Stakes or other training media may be used but should be unobtrusive.

Ornamental Foliage Plants These are either plants with foliage of a single colour or with foliage of two or more colours. Plants will be judged for foliage and general shape (according to the cultivar or species). Flowers will not be taken into consideration.

Individual Blooms Blooms must be clean, free from damage, disease or pests. Flowers should be typical in form and colour of the cultivar or species and in full bloom, complete with all floral parts. All floral parts, except the anthers, should be free of pollen.

Judges and Exhibitors Guidelines Cultural excellence and quality of growth are of prime importance.

•Prematurely opened buds, spent blooms, defoliated expanses of lateral growth and discoloured or damaged leaves detract from perfection and will be penalised accordingly.

•Flowers will be appraised on their state of perfection and must be typical in size, colour and form for the particular cultivar or species.

•The quality and distribution of flowers must be appropriate to the species or cultivar concerned.

•General grooming and presentation are important factors in close and difficult decisions.

•Containers must be clean and soil surfaces free of moss, weed, dead flowers and leaves or other debris.

•Plants must be in proportion to the size of the container.

•Stakes and ties, if used, must be inconspicuous and neat.

•Plants must be free of pests and diseases. Plants with obvious infestation will not be permitted in the Show, and if found, will be removed.

Below:
Dollar Princess is Allan's show banker for the doubles classes. With red-and-purple blooms, it never fails to oblige

Right:
This very hardy cultivar, Margaret Brown, is named after one of our leading fuchsia authorities, Mrs Margaret Slater. It makes an excellent, free-flowering hedge and is ideal for the hardy show class

SHOW DEFINITIONS AS USED IN THE BRITISH FUCHSIA SOCIETY'S SHOWS

A   A Full Standard shall be not less than 30in (762mm) and not more than 43in (1067mm).

A Half Standard shall be not less than 18in (457mm) and not more than 30in (762mm).

A Quarter Standard shall be not less than 10in (254mm) nor exceed 18in (457mm).

A Mini Standard shall be not less than 6in (152mm) nor exceed 10in (254mm).

These dimensions refer to the length of clear stem between the top of the compost and the underside of the lowest branch.

B   A **bush** is a plant which may be grown on a single stem not exceeding 1½in (38mm) in length or on shoots produced from below soil level.

C   **Standard Pots** must be used, ie the inside diameter of the pot should be approximate to the perpendicular height, and the diameter at the top should be appreciably greater than the diameter at the bottom (ie the pots should have a distinct taper). Half pots are not allowed.

D   **Size of Pots:** the diameter of a pot is the inside measurement as near to the top as possible, but without including any part of the roll of the rim.

E   **A Full Basket** must be of hemispherical shape, and a **Half Basket** of demi-hemi-spherical shape, ie straight sided baskets are not allowed.

F   **Encliandra Types** are those sometimes referred to as *Breviflorae* and have their origins in the section *Encliandra*.

G   **Triphylla Types** are plants similar to *F. Triphylla* with terminal flowers. The practice of exhibiting *Triphylla* types in the classes reserved for singles has been discussed by the BFS. For an experimental period *Triphylla* types will be confined to the classes reserved for them at the BFS Shows. However, it has been agreed that *Triphylla* types may continue to be exhibited in the Standard, Hanging Basket, Wall Basket and Hanging Pot Classes.

H   **A Beginner** is a Competitor who has not won a First, Second or Third Prize at any previous BFS Show.

I   **A Novice** is a Competitor who has not won a First Prize, with the exception of a Beginners Class, at any previous BFS Show.

J   **A Fuchsia** for Show purposes should have four sepals. It is however appreciated that some cultivars habitually throw blooms with more or less than four sepals and this should not be treated as a cultural fault.

A **Single** flowered fuchsia for show purposes shall have four petals only.

A **Semi-Double** flowered fuchsia has from five to seven petals.

A **Double** flowered fuchsia has eight or more petals.

Semi-double flowered fuchsias should be exhibited in classes with **Single** flowered fuchsias.

K   **Cultivar** is the internationally accepted term for what was formerly known as a variety.

L   **Small Pot Culture** Please refer to the *Judges and Exhibitors Handbook*.

M   **Hanging Pots** In classes for Hanging Pots only commercially produced hanging pots will be permitted.

TYPES OF FLOWER

SINGLES

A typical medium sized flower of a single-type bloom. This cultivar is Sandboy. It has a carmine tube with carmine sepals, whilst the corolla is of purple with light carmine at the base. The filaments are cerise with the style cerise pink. One of the very few fuchsias which could be considered as a houseplant. The foliage is medium green.

SEMI-DOUBLES

Rose of Denmark is typical of a cultivar classed as either a single or semi-double. Note the petaloid at the base of the corolla. The tube is white as are the sepals on top, but they are flushed pink underneath and tipped green. The rosy mauve corolla is pink at the base and veined rose. Set off against the medium green foliage are the pink filaments and white style.

DOUBLES

Sonata is a typical example of a fully double, small to medium sized bloom. The tube is greenish white and the sepals are pink, paling to a green tip. The corolla is white veined pink and the filaments and style are pale pink. Foliage is medium green.

One of the upward looking cultivars which prove very attractive and showy, this is Pink Bon Accord. A single flower again. The tube is pale pink as are the sepals, but the latter are a deeper pink underneath and are tipped green. The corolla is rose pink and is paler at the base. The filaments are again rose pink and the style is pale pink. Foliage is medium green.

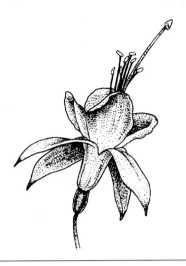

A smaller flowered semi-double, Saxondale, one ideal for bedding out in the front of the border. The tubes and sepals are crimson and the rose pink corolla is veined carmine. The filaments and style are also carmine. The flowers are shown to advantage against the medium green foliage.

The cultivar Pink Chiffon is an example of tighter form of double-flowered fuchsia. The tube is white with faint pink streaks, whilst the sepals are white tipped green. The corolla is of the very palest pink and the filaments are pale pink. The foliage is a lovely medium green colour.

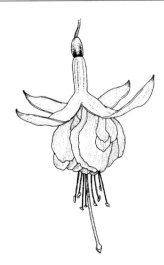

9

Tender Species and their Hybrids

There are in excess of one hundred species of *Fuchsia*. While many are attractive and often curious plants, relatively few are in general cultivation. Those and their progeny which are recorded here are obtainable in the British Isles and respond satisfactorily to cultivation under conditions which most home gardeners are able to provide. The countries listed refer to countries of origin. For explanations of botanical terms see Appendix 2; for abbreviations, p173.

THE SPECIES

Fuchsia ampliata See *F. ayavancensis.*

F. apiculata See *F. loxensis.*

F. arborescens (syn. F. syringaeflora). A low shrub, or in its natural habitat a small tree. Flowers numerous, in crowded panicles. Tube red to magenta; sepals purple; corolla lavender. Filament lavender-pink, purple anthers. Bold, glabrous, oblong-elliptic foliage with reddish veins. Mexico, Costa Rica, Panama and Guatamala. (1865, Sims)

F.a. forma parva Tube and sepals shorter than those of the species.

F.a. forma tenuis Tube and sepals narrower than those of the species.

F.a. forma typica Tube wider than that of the species.

All the above except *F. ampliata* are amenable to cultivation in a free-draining, fibrous compost. Equal parts moss peat and John Innes Potting Compost No 3 is ideal. They make useful specimens for standing outside during the summer months.

F. ayavancensis (syn. F. ampliata) A scrambling, shrubby plant. Tube and sepals deep red; corolla scarlet. Reflexed, spreading sepals and rounded, crimson petals. Leaves dark green above, pale beneath. Young shoots with a purplish cast. Peru and Ecuador. (1923, Kris)

Benefits from greenhouse cultivation. Grow in John Innes Potting Compost No 3. Does not prosper in the open in the north, even for the summer months.

F. boliviana A bushy shrub, forming a permanent framework of branches 0.9-1.8m (3-6ft) tall. Flowers produced in lax terminal panicles. Tube dark red; sepals spreading, reflexed, dark red; corolla pale red. Long, narrow blossoms often followed by fruits. Leaves elliptic with serrated margins, very downy when young, sparsely so when mature. Bolivia. (1876, Carr)

F.b. var. typica As the species, but decidedly hairy. Peru to Argentina.

Of easy cultivation in John Innes Potting Compost No 3 in a heated greenhouse. For the best results it demands a minimum night temperature of 15°C (60°F), although it will tolerate lower.

F. canescens (syn. F. vulcanica) A rangy, much-branched species with axillary blossoms. Tube scarlet with a purplish base. Sepals deep scarlet; corolla scarlet. Leaves dark green above, paler beneath. Colombia and Ecuador. (1845, Bentham)

A greenhouse species which grows satisfactorily in John Innes Potting Compost No 3. Best provided with some kind of permanent support or replaced regularly from cuttings.

Opposite:
F. boliviana. As the name implies, this is a true species found in Bolivia. It really needs that extra heat – on no account must it be grown cold

Below:
This is F. arborescens, a species which is also nicknamed the 'lilac fuchsia' – the flower-heads resemble those of the lilac. On the other hand, the leaves are very much like those of the laurel! In its native Central America it can grow up to 30ft in height, but in cooler climes needs extra warmth to succeed

F. coccinea (syn. F. elegans) This species can be grown in a sheltered spot outside in much of the country, but has not proved to be hardy at Harlow Car as yet. A pleasing plant, somewhat similar to *F. magellanica* (see Chapter 2). Tube and sepals red; corolla violet-purple. Upright habit with medium-sized, green leaves on reddish stems. Brazil. (1789, Soland)

Grow in the same way as a hardy cultivar in the south. Treat as a pot plant in the north.

F. confertifolia (syn. F. dolicantha) Not a very inspiring plant to look at, but an interesting one nevertheless. A rather gaunt, sparsely clothed individual with a summer scattering of pendant blossoms. Tube and sepals red with greenish flush; corolla red. The tube has a narrow base, widening suddenly for about two-thirds of its length. Small, oblong-ovate, green leaves with hairy veination beneath. Young growth somewhat downy. Peru and Brazil. (1844, Fielding and Gardner)

Grow as a greenhouse plant using John Innes Potting Compost No 3 as a growing medium.

F. cordifolia Very similar in many respects to *F. splendens* (see below), but more untidy and straggling. Flowers similar to those of *F. splendens,* but with stamens that barely protrude beyond the tube. The flowers are solitary in the upper axils. Tube deep scarlet; sepals scarlet with green tips; corolla green, yellow and white. Leaves almost as wide as long, cordate to ovate, with pale green undersides; young growth reddish. Guatemala. (1841, Bentham)

Requires regular greenhouse treatment. Grow in John Innes Potting Compost No 3.

F. corymbiflora (syn. F. dependens) A scrambling plant that is ideal for cultivation against the back wall of a lean-to greenhouse or up a pillar inside. Elegant, long blossoms borne in large, terminal racemes from a somewhat leggy, sparsely branched shrub. Tube and sepals scarlet; corolla coral-red. Large, softly pubescent, oblong-lanceolate leaves with long petioles. Peru. (1802, Ruiz and Pavon)

A good conservatory plant, especially if it can be planted into a greenhouse border with unrestricted root run. In pots use John Innes Potting Compost No 3.

F. denticulata (syn. F. grandiflora) A splendid, autumn-flowering, upright shrub with a potential to attain tree-like proportions, but in most collections is maintained as a rather large pot plant. Flowers later than most species. Tube and sepals reddish-pink, tipped with green; corolla red. Large, elliptic to oblong, somewhat fleshy leaves with distinctive, bright-green, upper surfaces, lighter undersides. Peru and Bolivia. (1802, Ruiz and Pavon)

Grow as a pot-grown shrub in the greenhouse using John Innes Potting Compost No 3. To get the best out of this plant it requires warmth during the autumn, particularly throughout the flowering period. Small plants do tolerably well in the home.

F. dependens See *F. corymbiflora.*

F. dolicantha See *F. confertifolia.*

F. elegans See *F. coccinea.*

F. encliandra (syn. F. parviflora) A shrubby plant with finely serrated foliage and tiny, reddish flowers. Tube and sepals red; corolla purplish-red. Mexico. (1840)

Treat as a greenhouse pot plant, growing in John Innes Potting Compost No 3. Pinch back regularly to maintain a reasonable habit.

F. excorticata This is one of the hardiest of the greenhouse species. In the wild it attains tree-like proportions, but under cultivation in this country forms a sizeable shrubby pot plant. Most interesting, small flowers; the tube and sepals open green and then turn purplish. Corolla dark purple to satiny black. Blue anthers. Foliage glossy green above, shiny white beneath. New Zealand. (1776, Forster)

Treat as a pot plant in greenhouse or sunlounge. Grow in John Innes Potting Compost No 3.

F. fulgens A shrubby plant 90cm (3ft) or more high with roots of a somewhat tuberous appearance. A handsome flowered species with long, pendulous blossoms borne in terminal racemes. Tube red; sepals yellowish or greenish; corolla vermilion. The conspicuous style is pink; the stigma greenish. Leaves are larger, hairy and of a light grey-green colour. Mexico. (1828, De Candolle)

This is considered to be a more or less epiphytic species and grows best in John Innes Potting Compost No 3 with about equal quantities by volume of coarse moss peat. A not unusual species that sometimes makes an appearance on the show bench.

Right:
F. loxensis, *a species with terminal buds flowering at the branch ends. Both this and* F. cordifolia *show the presence of* F. triphylla *in their history*

Above:
F. cordifolia. *A lovely picture of a species fuchsia, from which enthusiasts derive a great deal of pleasure. Note the flowers growing all along the length of the stem*

F.f. var. gesneriana Of more open and lax habit than the species, this has similar blossoms with shorter tubes. Guatemala.

F. gehrigeri A scrambling shrub that can be trained more or less like a climber into the roof of the greenhouse. In any event the reddish-green, drooping branches require some support if grown in a pot. Not the most prolific flowering species, but a very interesting one with pendant, terminal clusters of dark red flowers. Tube, sepals and corolla are a consistent red colour. Leaves deep green, elliptic, with finely serrated edges. Venezuela. (1943, Munz)

Benefits from being kept growing through the winter. Indeed, in an unheated house it is difficult to protect the vulnerable branches, especially when it

is grown as a climber or scrambler. It is perfectly happy in John Innes Potting Compost No 3.

F. grandiflora See *F. denticulata.*

F. hemsleyana (syn. F. pulchella) Upright, shrubby plant with small flowers borne singly in the leaf axils. Tube, sepals and corolla purplish-pink. Almost hardy and well suited to the unheated greenhouse. Costa Rica, Panama. (1937, Woodson and Siebert)

F. integrifolia See *F. regia.*

F. loxensis (syn. F. apiculata) A curio that is found in some collections. A shrubby, upright plant with axillary blossoms that have an unusual, trumpet-like, flared tube. Tube deep red; sepals scarlet; corolla dull red. Leaves deep green, rather shiny and with distinctive red veins. Peru, Ecuador. (1823, Kris)

Essentially a greenhouse plant responding to warm conditions and prospering in John Innes Potting Compost No 3.

F. michoacanensis An upright shrub which, if left untrained, will become unruly. When tamed, a most attractive plant with small axillary blossoms. Tube and sepals red; corolla coral-red. Leaves elliptic or ovate, young shoots hairy. Costa Rica, Mexico. (1887, Sesse and Mocina)

Sometimes seen on the show bench. Grows well in John Innes Potting Compost No 3 and should be treated as a greenhouse plant.

F. microphylla A lovely, bushy little plant 30-60cm (1-2ft) high, with small, dark green, leathery leaves. Small flowers followed by deep purplish-black fruits, rather like small blackcurrants. Tube and sepals dark red; corolla rose. Mexico. (1823, Kris)

At Harlow Car Gardens this is used as a decorative conservatory plant and grown in John Innes

Potting Compost No 3. It spends its entire life in a greenhouse which is just frost-free. Although said by some to be hardy, we have not yet found it to be reliably so. It would doubtless enjoy spending the summer outdoors although, because of its stature and flower size, it would not make a very significant contribution to a mixed planting. For this reason we prefer to enjoy it indoors, on the staging, at waist level.

F. parviflora See *F. encliandra.*

F. procumbens (syn. F. prostrata) A curious, scrambling plant that superficially bears little resemblance to a fuchsia. Unusual, rounded or oval, soft green leaves on wiry stems which root freely as they scramble across the compost. Flowers small, upward pointing; tube greenish-yellow with reddish-flushed base; sepals green with purplish tips; no corolla; pollen blue. Fruits large, purple when ripe, but pinkish and green fruits are often seen on a plant at the same time. New Zealand. (1839, Cunnington)

Hardy in many places. At Harlow Car Gardens we have to grow this in the unheated and well-ventilated, alpine display house. Use John Innes Potting Compost No 3 and cultivate in a wide pan rather than a pot for the best effect. When showing it is more conventional and acceptable to use a pot.

F. prostrata See *F. procumbens.*

F. pulchella See *F. hemsleyana.*

F. regia (syn. F. integrifolia) A large, bold shrub, in nature attaining almost small tree-like proportions. Can be effectively confined to a large pot and grown loosely along the lines of a standard, but does need a good sturdy support. Rather small, solitary flowers in the upper axils. Tube and sepals red; corolla dark red. Leaves medium to large, green with reddish veins and often appearing in threes. Brazil. (1842, Gardner)

A member of the tiny-flowered Encliandra *group,* F. microphylla *has blooms which can appear red, pink or near white. They are followed by dark berries that contrast well with the foliage*

F.r. var. alpestris Often referred to as *F. alpestris* by the horticultural trade. Similar to the species, but somewhat smaller.

F.r. var. radicans Flowers have a longer tube and shorter sepals. Glabrous foliage.

F.r. var. typica A compact form with more glabrous foliage, otherwise very similar to the species.

All the *F. regia* varieties grow well in John Innes Potting Compost No 3. While essentially greenhouse plants, they can be placed outside for the summer.

F. rivularis A rambling, shrubby plant with flowers borne singly in the leaf axils. Tube and sepals dark red; corolla purple and red. More or less ovate, green leaves, shiny above, downy beneath. Peru. (1940, Macbride)

A greenhouse plant similar in many ways to *F. canescens* (see above) and prospering in John Innes Potting Compost No 3.

F. sanctae-rosae Shrubby or sometimes almost herbaceous plant of a rather unruly, scandent habit. Flowers borne singly in the upper axils. Tube red; sepals scarlet; corolla orange-scarlet. Leaves produced in whorls of three or four. Bolivia, Peru. (1898, Kuntze)

A greenhouse subject that needs careful training to keep it in order. Grow in John Innes Potting Compost No 3.

F. simplicicaulis A rather vigorous, upright shrub which needs support. Flowers borne in pendulous racemes of green bracts, one blossom to each axil. Long, linear, lanceolate leaves. Peru. (1802, Ruiz and Pavon)

A greenhouse species which grows satisfactorily in John Innes Potting Compost No 3.

F. splendens One of the tougher species, which is allegedly hardy in some gardens, but certainly not at

TRIPHYLLA TYPE FUCHSIAS

The *triphylla* type fuchsias (such as Thalia) with their long, mostly red or orange flowers, provide a completely different flower type and colour. The flowerheads grow in panicles at the branch tips and continue to flower until the late autumn. If grown indoors, it is possible to have a plant in flower on the table on Christmas Day. The drawing shows a *triphylla* type fuchsia grown as a bush.

Harlow Car. A vigorous, pendant shrub with flowers borne either solitarily in the axils or crowded on short, lateral branches. Tube scarlet; sepals reddish and greenish-yellow; corolla green. The stamens are exserted (protruding). Large, green, cordate or ovate leaves. Costa Rica, Mexico. (1832, Zuccarini)

Quite a respectable and frequent flowerer when confined to pots. Use John Innes Potting Compost No 3.

F. syringaeflora See *F. arborescens*.

F. thymifolia Very similar to *F. microphylla* (see above), but with generally paler, more open, funnel-shaped blossoms. Flowers borne solitarily in the leaf axils. Tube white; sepals pinkish-white; corolla pinkish-white. Small, more or less ovate, green leaves; young growth reddish. Mexico. (1823, Kris)

Grows easily in a sunlounge or porch. Hardy in many areas, but not reliably so at Harlow Car.

F. triphylla Although very rarely seen in cultivation, this is worthy of a mention as the forerunner of the *triphylla* hybrids (see below) and the plant – under the name of *F. triphylla flore coccinae* – which Plumier used to found the genus *Fuchsia*. A very tender plant with long, tubed blossoms produced in dense terminal racemes. Tube, sepals and corolla red. Leaves copper to bronze with a reddish-purple cast beneath. San Domingo. (1703, Plumier)

Cultivars derived from this and unions with *F. fulgens, F. splendens* and *F. corymbiflora* (for all three, see above) all grow well in John Innes Potting Compost No 3. These cultivars constitute the *triphylla* hybrids and what is often referred to as *F. triphylla* by the trade.

F. vulcanica See *F. canescens*.

SPECIES HYBRIDS

There are many species hybrids (ie derived from species, rather than hybrid parents), but all those recorded here are reasonably freely available and are Allan's personal recommendation for both general decorative use and, where appropriate, show work. See below for an explanation of the abbreviations used.

Andenken an Heinrich Henkel

(syn. Heinrich Henkel) *(F. triphylla x)*

Single. Tube long, rosy-crimson; sepals and corolla crimson. Dark green, round foliage with a reddish cast. Flowers produced in long terminal racemes.

Ariel

(F. encliandra x F. hemsleyana)

Single. Tube magenta, spreading and distinctly pointed. Corolla deep magenta-pink. Flowers small, prolific and borne amongst tiny, bright green foliage. Upright habit. Can be trained to most shapes and easily accommodated in John Innes Potting Compost No 3. (1970, Travis)

Billy Green
(F. triphylla x)
Single. Tube long, salmon-pink, self coloured. Olive green foliage; upright habit. An important show cultivar. (1966)

Gartenmeister Bonstedt
(F. triphylla x)
Single. Tube long; entire flower orange and of similar appearance to Thalia (see below). Dark bronze-red foliage on a plant of upright habit. (1905, Bonstedt) (HC, 1929)

Heinrich Henkel See Andenken an Heinrich Henkel.

Koralle
(F. triphylla x)
Single. Tube long, salmon-orange; sepals salmon-orange; petals short, salmon-orange. Deep green leaves with a satiny texture and a bluish flush. Upright habit. Often referred to as 'Coralle'. Benefits from shading during hot weather. (1905, Bonstedt) (AM, 1929)

Lechlade Apache
(F. simplicicaulis X F. boliviana)
Single. Tube very long and thin, red; sepals recurved, red; corolla red. Foliage mid-green with maroon petioles. Stems with a maroon or purplish cast. Essentially a greenhouse plant. Much neater habit than either of its parents. Free-flowering, with blossoms in terminal racemes. (1984, Wright)

Lechlade Chinaman
(F. splendens X F. procumbens)
Single. Somewhat bizarre amber blossoms and a trailing habit. Useful for basket work. Requires greenhouse culture. (1938, Wright)

Lechlade Rajah
(F. boliviana X F. excorticata)
Single. Another strange species hybrid with long purple flowers. Must have greenhouse protection. (1938, Wright)

Lechlade Tinkerbell
(F. arborescens X F. thymifolia subsp. thymifolia)
   Single. A vigorous-growing *Encliandra* type (see
Appendix 1) with small pink flowers. (1983, Wright)

Mary
(F. triphylla X F. corymbiflora)
   Single. Tube long, bright scarlet; sepals scarlet,

Thalia is still the best of the triphylla *types, sporting tubular orange-red flowers and dark green foliage with a deep red underside. But watch out – whitefly love it!*

reflexed; corolla scarlet. Foliage dark green, heavily ribbed. Dark red veins, purplish undersides. (1894, Bonstedt)

Neapolitan
(Encliandra type (see Appendix 1), exact origin unknown)
Single. A fuchsia with unstable chromosomes for flower colour, thus pink, red and white flowers appear on different parts of the plant at the same time. Individual blossoms are tiny with reflexed sepals. A novelty, probably the most bizarre fuchsia of all. (1984, Clark)

Pink Trumpet
(F. boliviana X F.b. luxurians)
Single. Tube long, pink; sepals white, reflexed; corolla red, petals falling prematurely. A very fine, large-flowered hybrid with handsome green foliage, larger than anything commonly seen in cultivated fuchsias. Strange, green, egg-shaped fruits, with red stippling. Makes a fine standard. (1981, Wright)

Speciosa
(F. splendens X F. fulgens)
Single. Closely resembling *F. fulgens* (see above), but with shorter-tubed flowers of orange-red, much more freely produced.

Thalia
(F. triphylla x)
Single. Tube long, orange-scarlet; sepals small, orange-scarlet; corolla orange-scarlet. Flowers borne in heavy terminal racemes. Upright growth habit with handsome soft foliage of deep olive-green to maroon.

The most popular of the *triphylla* (see above) hybrids. Not infrequently seen offered as a houseplant by garden centres. Can also be used to good effect for bedding. (1905, Bonstedt)

Waldfee

(F. michoacanensis x)

Single. Tube long, spreading, lilac-pink; sepals lilac-pink; corolla reflexed, lilac-pink. Small flowers very freely produced. Growth upright; foliage small and green. (1973, Travis)

White Knights Amethyst

(F. magellanica X F. excorticata)

Single. Tube reddish-purple; sepals pale reddish-purple to yellow-green; corolla violet to reddish-purple. Small, dark green foliage and upright bushy growth. Ideal for training as a pillar or pyramid. Allegedly hardy in parts of the south of Britain, as yet untried in the north. (1980, Wright)

White Knights Goblin

(F. denticulata)

Single. Tube long, crimson, widening at the mouth; sepals green; corolla scarlet. A beautiful, large-flowered cultivar which resulted from a batch of South American seed. A natural variation which is propagated vegetatively. Leaves dark green with reddish-brown undersides and veins. Must have year-round greenhouse cultivation to give of its best. (1981, Wright)

AM   Award of Merit of the Royal Horticultural Society.

HC   Highly Commended by the Royal Horticul tural Society.

10
Fuchsia Cultivars

It is not our intention here to produce a catalogue of all the fuchsia cultivars currently available. The purpose of this chapter is to make a selection of those that are suited to different purposes, whether in the home or garden, or on the show bench.

In this chapter * indicates cultivars especially recommended by Allan both for general decoration and for showing. Many have been grown by him under typical home-garden conditions — a 3.5 x 2.5m (12 x 8ft) greenhouse and a standing-out area — yet he has won the top awards in the fuchsia world with these plants. See Appendix 2 for explanations of botanical terms.

Abbe Farges Semi-double. A favourite and very hardy, smaller-flowered plant. Light cerise reflexed sepals and tube; corolla lilac-rose. Small, medium green foliage. Stems very brittle, but excellent garden, greenhouse and show plant when skilfully grown. Improves in its third and fourth year. (1901, Lemoine)

Opposite:
Blue Waves. One of the best of the large-flowered USA-bred doubles, it usually avoids the common problem of these cultivars whereby the flowers tend to flare outwards, like a full-blown rose

Alf Thornley Double. Shortish pink tube; creamy-white double corolla of near perfect shape. Mid-green foliage. Very floriferous, well-shaped plant, often producing two flowers per leaf axil. Recommended for beginners. Grown extensively in the north. (1981, Clark)

*****Alison Reynolds** Double. Tube rose-bengal; sepals

rose-bengal shading to pink and cream, with green tips; corolla violet. Medium-sized flowers with pink stamens and white pistil. Leaves small to medium, green. Recommended as a shrub or bush. (1982, Reynolds)

*__Alwin__ Semi-double. Tube rose; sepals rose. Together they form a short thick tube with the sepals reflexed. Corolla fluted, white with red veins. Medium-sized blossoms. Recommended as a shrub or bush. Ideal for small pot classes. (1976, Clyne)

*__Amanda Jones__ Single. Tube somewhat bulbous, white with pink flush; sepals white, flushed with pink, rose beneath. Corolla mauve-pink. Light green ovate or cordate foliage. Growth upright. Recommended as a shrub or bush. (1981)

__Amy Lye__ Single. Tube cream; sepals white with green tips; corolla orange. Medium-sized blossoms, early. Leaves dark green with prominent red mid-rib. Recommended as a standard. (1885, Lye)

*__Angela Rippon__ Single. Tube china-rose; sepals china-rose with green tips; corolla wisteria-blue to purple. Medium-sized blossoms on a lusty, short-jointed, self-branching plant. (1977, Gadsby)

*__Anna of Longleat__ Single. Tube pale red; sepals pale red, corolla pale pinkish-red. Small leaves on short-jointed stems. Ideal for small pots, hanging pots and baskets, as it is self shaping.

*__Annabel__ Double. Tube long, white, striped with pink; sepals white, flushed with pink with curled tips; double corolla white, veined with pink. Pink stamens and light pink style. Growth upright, leaves pale green. (1977, Ryle)

*__Ann Howard Tripp__ Single to semi-double. Tube short and thick, white with faint stripe; sepals white, tinged with pink and with green tips; corolla white, veined pink. Produces two flowers in each leaf axil. Upright growth, self-branching. Recommended for shrub or bush. (1982, Clark)

* **Atlantic Star** Single. Tube, sepals and corolla white, shaded pink. Medium-flowered, short-jointed growth with green leaves veined red. Recommended as a shrub or bush. (Redfern)

* **Auntie Jinks** Single. Tube reddish-pink; sepals white, edged with cerise, corolla reddish-purple with white shading. Pink style and pale pink filaments. Small blossoms and smallish green leaves. Lax growth. Ideal for small pot culture or a hanging basket. (1970, Wilson)

* **Autumnale** Single. Tube and sepals scarlet-pink; corolla purple. Medium-sized flowers, rather late. Small, smooth, shiny leaves, golden and coppery-red. Difficult to train to a defined shape because of its more or less horizontal growth habit. (*c*1880)

* **Ballet Girl** Double. Tube and sepals cerise; corolla white. Sepals reflexed with fully double corolla. Growth upright. Makes a good bush or standard. (1894, Veitch) (AM, 1929)

* **Barbara** Single. Tube short, pale pink; sepals pale pink and upturned at tips; corolla cherry and tangerine-pink. Leaves medium sized, pale green. Especially recommended for training as a standard, but not at its best until three or more years old. Also makes a good pyramid, pillar or conical shape. (1971, Tolley)

* **Beacon** Single. Deep pink tube and sepals glow against the bright mauve corolla. Floriferous, strong-growing plant with leaves a darker green (indicating resistance to disease and damping off and, usually, a good degree of hardiness). Recommended for show bench or garden, and will make an excellent bush or standard (1871, Bull)

* **Beacon Rosa** Single. Tube long, pinkish-red; sepals

pink-red; corolla pink, veined with red. Dark green leaves with waved edges. Recommended as a shrub or bush. (1972, Burgi-Ott)

*Bealings** Double. Tube white; sepals white, but producing a pinkish flush with age. Corolla violet. Very free flowering with medium-sized blossoms. Small green leaves. Suffers from botrytis if not carefully watered. (1983, Goulding)

Beauty of Trowbridge Single. Tube and sepals thick, waxy and creamy-white. Corolla bright cerise-rose. Beautifully shaped flowers appear in abundance. Best grown as a large bush or standard plant, inside or out, as even in wet weather the blooms will stand out in their elegance. A quality fuchsia with a great tradition, very much in line with the James Lye cultivars. (c1879)

Bernadette Double. Tube and sepals pale rose; corolla blue with mauvish cast. Medium-sized blossoms amongst small, dark green leaves. Growth very neat and upright. (1950, Schnabel)

*Blue Bush** Single. Sepals and tube rosy red; corolla opens a beautiful bluebird blue, fading to a distinct violet blue. Flowers medium sized, produced on a vigorous upright bush. Best grown as a hardy, and ideal for a hedge 5-6ft high, when given the best of situations and cultivation. (1973, Gadsby)

Opposite;
Border Queen, a superb single cultivar which is very adaptable. A winner everywhere as a bush or hanging basket, when grown as a standard by showman Mal Wilkinson of Grimsby it is a champion every time. But can anyone truthfully distinguish it from its twin, Eden Lady?

Blue Waves Double. Tube short, pale pink; sepals upturned, rose. Corolla violet. Large blossoms on a sturdy plant of upright habit. Makes a good standard. (1954, Waltz)

*Blush Of Dawn** Double. Tube white; sepals white with green tips; corolla silvery-grey and lavender-blue. Free flowering, but rather late. A good exhibition cultivar, but the flowers are easily damaged in transit. Very useful for a basket or half basket. Foliage green. (1962, Martin)

*Bobby Shaftoe Semi-double. Tube short, white, flushed with pink; sepals white, flushed with pink with yellowish tips. Corolla white, blushed pink and with pink veins. Growth upright, self branching. Leaves oval, shiny, light green. Prone to botrytis, but nevertheless a superb cultivar. (1973, Ryle-Atkinson)

*Bon Accorde Single. Tube and sepals white; corolla pale purple suffused with white. Flowers small, borne in a stiff, more or less erect fashion. Becomes leggy if confined to the greenhouse. Requires constant pinching back for the show bench. (1861, Crousse)

*Border Queen Single. Tube short, pink; sepals pink, tipped with green; corolla violet, flushed with pink. Look out for extra petaloids. Leaves medium green, smooth; stems reddish. Upright, self-branching growth. Recommended for shrub, bush, hanging basket, standards, conical shapes, pyramids, pillars, espaliers or fans. A truly versatile cultivar. (1974, Ryle-Atkinson)

Bow Bells Single or semi-double. Tube short, white; sepals long, white; corolla red with a white base. Large, early flowerer with upright growth. (1972, Handley)

Brenda White Single. Tube and sepals carmine; corolla white. A smallish flower, this is a show variety. (1986)

*Bunny Semi-double. Tube and sepals cerise; corolla lilac-pink with violet-rose picotee (frilled) edge. Upright, bushy growth. Recommended for small pot culture and outdoor bedding. (1965, Need)

*Cambridge Louie Single. Tube and sepals orange-pink, darker beneath; corolla rose-pink with darker edges. Foliage small, light green. Appears to be a light-framed plant, but is really very strong. A good exhibition plant. (1977, Napthen)

Cascade Single. Tube white; sepals long, slender and white flushed with carmine; corolla deep carmine. Blossoms medium sized, but plentiful. Growth pendulous, making this the ideal plant for a hanging basket. (1937, Lagen)

*Celadore Double. Tube, sepals and corolla candy-pink, almost luminescent. Medium-sized blossoms amongst deep green, heart-shaped leaves. A naturally trailing cultivar and therefore well suited to hanging basket or weeping standard culture. (1981, Hall)

*Celia Smedley Single. Tube and sepals rose; corolla currant-red. Large flowers and bold green foliage. Growth vigorous and bushy, but the wood hardens rather too early for some growers. It is at its best after two or three years. Never show a young plant, even though it can attain a reasonable size in a single season. All the prizewinners are more mature plants. As this cultivar has a more vigorous root system than others, it can be allowed a much larger pot than normal, with a richly organic compost. Can be recommended for shrub, bush, pyramid, pillar or conical training. A truly outstanding plant. (1970, Roe)

Chang Single. Tube and sepals orange-red; tips of the sepals green paling to white; corolla a very brilliant orange. A smaller-flowered cultivar, with blooms produced in profusion on an upright bush. Requires plenty of pinching out to maintain shape. Botrytis can be troublesome, and it is therefore at its best summer planted in the border. (1946, Hazard and Hazard)

*Charming Single. Tube carmine; sepals reddish-cerise; corolla rose-purple with a cerise base. Medium-sized flowers in abundance on an upright, bushy plant. An easily grown and trained cultivar for the beginner. (1895, Lye)

Checkerboard Single. Long red tube flows into sepals which start red and then abruptly change to white; the deeper red corolla is white at its base. Must be contained by regular pinching, as it grows very quickly indeed. There are some excellent plants shown on the show bench. It produces its medium-sized flowers very, very profusely; it is early and is always in bloom despite the ever falling flowers. Recommended as a pyramid or conical; also makes an ideal standard. (1948, Walker and Jones)

Chillerton Beauty Single. Pale rose-red tube and sepals both tipped green; corolla mauve-violet veined pink. Medium-sized blooms; floriferous. A good, upright, strong grower ideal for the smaller hedge. (1847, Bass)

*****Cloth Of Gold** Single. Tube and sepals red; corolla purple. Small to medium blossoms, sparsely produced. It is for its golden and bronze-flushed foliage that this is grown. A very useful exhibition foliage cultivar. A bushy little plant. (1863, Stafford)

Cloverdale Jewel Semi-double. Neyron rose sepals held well back from a similarly coloured tube; corolla a colourful wisteria blue with rose veining, fading to violet blue. Beautiful, medium-sized blooms on a strong-growing plant that responds well to pinching out. With one of its parents being Lady Isobel Barnet, one can appreciate what to expect from it. (1974, Gadsby)

*****Cloverdale Pearl** Single. Tube white; sepals pink shading to white, with green tips, reflexed; corolla white. Bushy habit, self-branching. (1979, Gadsby)

*****Coquet Belle** Single or semi-double. No matter how it is grown it can make an absolutely stunning plant. It is also a good one for the beginner. Short tube and sepals rose madder, tipped green; medium-sized, slightly waved, bell-shaped flowers pale mauve flushed rose with red veining. Medium-sized, mid-green leaves. Upright, self-branching and free flowering with a parentage of Lena Dalton x Citation. Excellent however it is grown. Recommended for the beginner. (1973, Ryle-Atkinson)

Corallina Single. Rich purple corolla, scarlet tube and sepals. Mid to darkish green leaves, slightly larger than normal. A really hardy, strong grower with naturally spreading growth. As a hedge will reach about 90cm (3ft). Ideal for the front of a shrubbery border. (1844, Pince)

Countess of Aberdeen Single. Tube and sepals pale pink; corolla creamy-white fading to pale pink in shade, rich pink when grown out of doors. A neat and tidy, upright growing bush. Leaves medium green, small in size. A beautiful smaller-flowered cultivar, ideal for 8.5cm (3½in) pot class but not easy to grow. Susceptible to botrytis – a 'must' for testing your skills. (1888, Dobbie-Forbes)

Crosby Soroptimist Single. Tube and sepals rhodamine pink; corolla white. Foliage dark green, giving a good contrast with the flowers. A very free flowering plant of good substance. (D. Clark)

*Daisy Bell Single. Tube long, white with an orange flush; sepals pale orange shading to green at the tips; corolla vermilion shading to orange at the base. A naturally trailing cultivar that is ideal for baskets and half baskets. Makes a neat plant with the minimum of pinching. (1977)

*Dark Eyes Double. Tube short, deep red; sepals upturned, deep red; corolla violet-blue with the petals curled. Free-flowering, medium-sized blossoms on an upright plant. One of the easiest doubles to prepare for show. A good beginner's cultivar. (1958, Erickson)

Dark Secret Double. Tube short, greenish; sepals, broad and upturned, white outside, pinkish within; corolla deep violet with an occasional pink flush.

Blossoms medium sized and borne amongst dark green foliage on a plant of upright habit. (1957, Hodges)

*D-Day 44 Double. Tube cream; sepals large, white with a pink outer edge; corolla white, veined with pink; stamens bright red. Foliage mid-green, the edges of the leaves serrated. Upright growth habit. Recommended for bush, shrub or standard growth as well as for bedding out in the garden. (1985, Redfern)

*Delicia Single. Tube short, white; sepals crimson and white with recurved tips; corolla purple. Ovate green leaves on magenta stems. Bushy habit. Recommended for training as a bush, shrub or standard. (1984, Redfern)

*Derby Imp Single. Tube narrow, crimson; sepals crimson, rosy-red beneath; corolla violet-blue to violet. Flowers small, elegant and produced in large quantities. Leaves small, green and carried on wiry stems. A naturally scrambling cultivar that is ideal for baskets and small pots. (1974, Gadsby) ·

Display Single. Almost self pink, the corolla a little deeper than the tube and sepals. Medium green, healthy foliage. Early to flower, very floriferous and continues to the end of the season. Needs very little training to form any shape. Ideal for the show-bench, greenhouse or summer bedding. Recommended for beginners. (1881, Smith)

*Dollar Princess Double. Tube and sepals cerise; corolla purple. Smaller flowers than usual for a double, but produced in abundance. Growth both vigorous and upright lending itself to training in almost all the defined forms. An easygoing, old-fashioned cultivar that every beginner should try. (1912, Lemoine)

*Doreen Redfern Single. Tube short, white; sepals white above, lilac beneath, tips green; corolla violet.

Filaments and anthers pale lilac; style and stigma white. Leaves cordate, dark green with pale greenish-white veins and stems. Growth upright. Recommended for bush or standard cultivation. (1984, Redfern)

*Dulcie Elizabeth Double. Tube rose; sepals reflexed, rose; corolla powder-blue flecked with rose. Growth upright, bushy, self-branching. Foliage bright green. (1974, Clyne-Aimes)

*Dusky Beauty Single. Tube rose; sepals rose. Corolla pale purple with pink cast. Flowers small, but borne in abundance amongst dark green foliage. Growth upright. Recommended for bush or shrub. Flourishes in small pots. (1981, Ryle)

*Eden Lady Single. Tube short, thin, pale rose; sepals rose; corolla blue with rose colouring at base of petals. Bright red stamens. Self-branching, upright habit. Adaptable to most modes of training, but especially recommended for bush and shrub culture. (1975, Ryle)

Eden Princess Single. Tube and sepals deep pink, nearly red; rich purple corolla; a medium-sized flower which contrasts beautifully with unusual yellow foliage. Upright, bushy grower, ideal for training into a standard of some substance. Recently introduced. (1984, Mitchinson)

*Edith Emery Semi-double. Tube short and thick, white; sepals reflexed, white; corolla violet. Short, compact flowers produced in quantity. Rather small, green foliage on a plant of upright habit. Self-branching and short-jointed. (1975, Clyne)

*Edna May Single. Tube striped pink and white; sepals white flushed with pink beneath; corolla cream. Anthers scarlet. Flowers medium sized, freely produced, exhibiting a fine scarlet edge to the sepals when grown in full light. Self-branching, bushy, with dark green foliage. (1982, Clark)

Eileen Saunders Single. Carmine tube veined crimson; crimson sepals tipped green, longer than most and reflexed back to cover the tube; corolla fuchsia purple with a carmine base veined crimson. The slightly bent tube of the flower gives this cultivar that extra appeal. Makes a good upright bush. Named after the author of 'The Wagtail Series' of fuchsia publications and to whom we are indebted for articles in the Species section of this book (1974, Holmes)

*Empress of Prussia Single. Tube and sepals bright scarlet; corolla magenta red, a little paler at the base. Blooms larger than medium-sized. Very hardy, outstanding for its profuse flowering. Strong upright growth, makes a good hedge of 90-120cm (3-4ft). (1868)

Estelle Marie Single. Tube short, thick, greenish-white; sepals white with green tips; corolla blue-violet with white towards the base of the petals. Leaves oval, dark green, on an upright self-branching plant. Prone to botrytis and not the easiest to shape. When well grown an absolute delight. Ideal for small pot culture. (1973, Newton)

*Eva Boerg Single to semi-double. Tube greenish-white; sepals white, flushed with pink, pink beneath; corolla pinkish-purple. A lax, low-growing bush. Excellent for a hanging basket. (1943, Yorke)

*Evensong Single. Tube white; sepals white with pinkish base; corolla white. Blossoms medium sized and borne amongst light green foliage. Growth bushy and upright. (1967, Colville)

*Falling Stars Single. Tube pale scarlet; sepals pleated, pale scarlet; corolla turkey-red with a hint of orange. Free flowering; upright, bushy habit; needs a lot of pinching to control its shape. A first-class standard. (1941, Reiter)

Bred by Fred Redfern and named after his wife, Doreen Redfern is one of the best of the many varieties he has introduced – Allan has judged it Best in Show in the past. Grow it as a bush or standard

Fanfare Single. Tube long, scarlet; sepals short, scarlet;

corolla short, turkey-red. An interesting, variable, late-blooming cultivar with exotic-looking blossoms. Vigorous, untidy growth supporting deep green leaves. (1941, Reiter)

Fire Mountain Double. Flesh-coloured tube with pale orange sepals; corolla orange carmine, more orange on outer petals. Medium green leaves fairly large, with reddish veins and stems on new growth. Strong growing; requires staking to prevent branches snapping off under the weight of bloom. Worth growing for its brilliance of colour. (1980, Stubbs)

*****Flirtation Waltz** Double. Tube white; wide, spreading sepals, white with pinkish flush; corolla shell-pink darkening with age. Medium-sized blossoms and vigorous, upright growth. The flowers bruise easily and tend to brown if kept in too damp an atmosphere. Excellent as a standard. (1962, Waltz)

*****Florence Mary Abbott** Single. Tube short, white with pink streaks; sepals white with pinkish flush; corolla pure white. Light green foliage with reddish mid-rib. Upright, short-jointed growth, self branching. One of the best whites for mildew resistance. Makes a good plant in a hanging pot. (1983, Goulding)

Fountains Abbey Double. White tube with pinkish-white sepals, tipped green; corolla a beautiful lavender blue flushed and veined pink. Medium green foliage. Growth lax, so ideal for basket work (makes a particularly lovely half basket). Bred near Harrogate and named after the famous abbey. (1981, Akers)

*****Frank Unsworth** Double. Almost a self white, corolla with just a touch of a pink flush. A quality flower, shown to perfection against the darker green leaves; produces extra blooms in the leaf axils. Perfect for a hanging pot or basket, and better than Harry Gray (see below) which is one of the best. Easy to grow, and recommended for beginners. (1982, Clark)

Garden News Double. Tube short, thick and pink; sepals short, pink; corolla magenta-rose. Large blossoms produced in pairs in the leaf axils. Foliage mid-green; growth tall and vigorous. This is currently undergoing hardiness trials at Harlow Car Gardens. A free-branching cultivar (ie it branches often without constant pinching) that is excellent as a bush or shrub. (1978, Handley)

Gartenmeister Bonstedt Single. A triphylla hybrid similar to the best triphylla Thalia, but slightly inferior. The long tube has a bulge in the middle, which distinguishes the two. Flowers orangey-red and produced in terminal racemes at the end of the branches. Foliage dark bronze: red underneath and more green on top. Growth upright and vigorous, but very frost shy. Go easy with the watering. Another for the table on Christmas Day. Recommended for beginners.

*Genii Single. Tube and sepals cerise; corolla rich violet fading to dark rose. Once in bloom it is never short of flower. Both the flowers and foliage are of the smaller size, but the length of the lovely crimson stamens and pistil when in full flower, and the golden colour of the leaves, make this one a must as a 'dot' or pot plant for the garden. Will also make a superb show specimen as a three year old plant in a 15cm (6in) pot. It does not like living indoors at all. Recommended for beginners, and one of the top hardy fuchsias. (1951, Reiter)

*Golden Marinka Single. Tube and sepals red; corolla dark red. A golden-yellow foliage sport from Marinka (see below). Probably the most popular foliage cultivar of all. Needs maximum light to produce the best colour. A useful basket plant. (1955, Weber)

*Golden Runner (Gold Runner) Single. Pale pink tube and sepals, paling at the tips; corolla a perfect rose-pink. Foliage variegated gold and green, colours best in full sun. A combination of a profuse flowering fuchsia with variegated leaves of natural size make this a winner for the variegated show class, where most plants have few flowers and are generally difficult to grow, mainly due to overwatering and botrytis problems. This one has no problems, makes an outstanding dot plant for the summer border and is recommended for beginners. (1984, Tolley)

Halsall Beauty Double. Tube pale rose pink; sepals white with a little pinking; corolla blue. A beautiful cultivar with medium-sized blooms. It holds the older flowers well, giving a two-tone effect between old and new colouring. (R. Sinton)

Harlow Car Single. Tube and sepals pink; corolla white. A completely new cultivar which we have been unable to assess fully yet, but which we must include here. It is unlikely to prove to be a first-class exhibition cultivar. (1987, Johns)

Harry Gray Double. Tube rose-pink; sepals slightly recurved, white shading to rose-pink at base, tips green; corolla white shading to rose-pink. Pink stamens and prominent white pistil. Small to medium-sized blossoms amongst small, dark green foliage. A self-branching, short-jointed plant of rather lax growth. Perfect for a hanging pot or basket. (1981, Dunnett)

Heidi Ann Double. Tube and sepals crimson cerise; corolla bright lilac veined cerise. Dark green leaves. An upright bushy plant which needs a few pinches, but creates no problems. A favourite on the show bench. Recommended for beginners. (1969, Smith)

Herald Single. Scarlet sepals recurve from a scarlet tube; corolla deep purple. Leaves darkish green and medium sized; plant upright and bushy. A very good, old hardy for the garden. Recommended for newcomers to the hardy show class. (1887, Sankey)

Iced Champagne is a beautiful flower. The growth is lax and the plant is ideally suited to basket work or the hanging pot classes. It takes some beating when well grown

Iceberg Single. Tube red striped carmine with red marked, reflexing white sepals; corolla white, medium sized and better grown in shade than in the open, where it will redden up. Darkish green leaves have well serrated edges. Growth upright and bushy, and can be trained into just about every shape.

*__*Icecap__* Single to semi-double. Tube and sepals cardinal-red; corolla white with red veins. Medium-sized blossoms amongst bushy, upright growth. A superb exhibition cultivar for shrub or bush culture. Also makes a good standard. (1968, Gadsby)

Iced Champagne Single. Tube and sepals dawn pink ageing to pale pink as the sepals turn upwards and towards the tube, reflexing. Rather long flowers are rhodamine pink and produced in profusion throughout the season. Short-jointed, and better grown naturally and not pinched out too much. Needs care and some expertise. (1968, Jennings)

Igloo Maid Double. Almost a self white; hint of pink in the corolla, sepals tipped green. Flowers larger sized, but this vigorous cultivar is not shy in producing them. Leaves a yellowish green making this bushy upright plant useful for contrast. (1972, Holmes)

Independence Double. Tube white with green markings; sepals long, sometimes twisted, pink; corolla currant-red. Large blossoms and medium-sized green leaves with conspicuous red veins. Growth upright; makes a good bush. (1976, Stubbs)

Isle of Mull Single. Tube light magenta with darker veining; sepals soft pink with deeper veining; corolla rose magenta with pinking towards the base. Tube short and thick, sepals not overlong, corolla medium sized – a quality flower, freely produced. Medium to dark green leaves on a short-jointed, upright-growing, bushy plant. Easy to grow; a minimum of pinching will produce a first class show specimen. In a summer bedding scheme or trough it will really show its best. (1978, Tolley)

*Jack Shahan Single. Tube and sepals pale rose-bengal; corolla rose-bengal. Large flowers freely produced amongst lax growth. An ideal hanging basket plant. (1948, Tiret)

*Jackie Bull Double. Tube long, shell-pink; sepals rose with a deeper veining; corolla lilac-mauve, often pinkish at base. Medium-sized blossoms and leaves of similar size, green, ovate. Upright bushy habit. (1985, Redfern)

Jean Clark Single. Tube rose-pink; sepals white with a tendency to pink when not in shade; corolla a delightful blue. Leaves and flowers small; an upright grower. This is one for the 9cm (3½in) pot class. (R. McDonald)

Jean Ewart Single. Rose coloured sepals fold back to the similarly coloured tube; corolla more of an amaranth rose. Small to medium-sized flowers, freely produced on a really good, upright, bushy plant. Leaves medium green and medium sized, in proportion to the plant. Suitable for quarter or half standard. Named after the current assistant secretary of the British Fuchsia Society. (1981, Roe)

*Jenny Sorenson Single. Tube and sepals red; corolla mauvish-white with heavy picotee edge. Upright, bushy growth. Ideal for training as either a bush or standard. (1988, Wilkinson)

*Joan Pacey Single. Tube long, white; sepals pink, tipped green; corolla purplish-pink, veined rose. Extremely free flowering with medium-sized blossoms. Growth habit bushy and upright. Best when allowed to develop fully, especially as an espalier. (1972, Gadsby)

*Joy Patmore Single. Tube short, white; sepals upturned, white with a hint of pink; corolla rich

One of the newer
cultivars from
Mal Wilkinson,
Jenny Sorenson is coming
into favour with
exhibitors. Its
outstanding feature is the
dark picotee edging to
each petal

carmine. Medium-sized blossoms, free flowering
and with bushy upright habit. (1961, Turner)

*June Gardner Single. Tube and sepals rose, the latter
tipped green; corolla deep purple fading to rose
towards the centre. Red stamens, carmine-rose
stigma. Golden foliage and a pleasing bushy habit.
It is ideal for growing as a standard, but does
demand full light if the distinctive foliage is to look
its best. A cultivar where the wood hardens quickly,
therefore an easy one to overwinter. (1982, Bielby)

*Ken Jennings Single. Tube short, thick, pink; sepals
pink; corolla Tyrian-purple. Flowers medium sized;
habit upright and bushy. A first-class bedding fuchsia. (1982, Roe)

Khada Single. Sepals and tube rose red; corolla white
veined rose. An ideal cultivar for the 9cm (3 ½in) pot

class being a floriferous, small-flowered, small-jointed and small-leaved plant. The first upward looking or horizontal red and white fuchsia produced – today we would like to see it paired up with Nellie Nuttall, a more recent fuchsia but one which is sure to be in the top rating for a long time to come. Easy to grow and cultivate and ideal for the summer rock garden. (1973, Roe)

King's Ransom Double. Tube white; sepals recurved, white; corolla deep purple. Medium-sized flowers on an upright-growing bush. (1954, Schnabel)

La Campanella Semi-double. Tube and sepals white, flushed with pink; corolla purple. Free flowering, with myriad small blossoms. Filaments bright pink, style pure white. A self-branching plant with small, green leaves. Recommended for quarter and half standards and baskets as well as fans, espaliers and small pot classes. (1968, Blackwell)

*****Lady Dorothy** Single. Tube, sepals, corolla, bright vermilion red. Handsome, dark green foliage of similar habit to Beacon Rosa (see pp 177-8) from which it is a sport. (1960, Robinson)

*****Lady Isobel Barnett** Single. Tube and sepals rosy red; corolla rose-purple with edges flushed purple. Blossoms small or medium sized, borne semi-erect on a plant of upright, bushy habit. Recommended for small pot and conical culture. It is prone to botrytis. (1968, Gadsby)

*****Lady Patricia Mountbatten** Single. Tube and sepals whitish to pale pink; corolla pale lilac. A neat, compact, bushy plant. Appears to have tremendous potential for the show bench. (1985, Clark)

*****Lady Ramsey** Single. Tube short, flesh-pink; sepals flesh-pink, somewhat reflexed; corolla violet, almost bell shaped. Two or three medium-sized flowers to each leaf joint. Self-branching growth with medium-sized, green leaves. Makes a good basket, bush or standard. (1981, Goulding)

*Lady Thumb Semi-double. Tube and sepals carmine red; corolla white veined carmine. Small-leaved, free flowering and very hardy. Its small size makes it ideal for the rockery or for border edging. At Harlow Car it excels itself and makes a lovely hummock or red and white. Ideal for 9cm (3 ½in) pot work and perfect for attempting the bonsai type of growth. A fault of the Thumb family is that the sepals do not open up to the full horizontal and tend to hide the corolla, but this may be an advantage in an outdoor fuchsia as the downward sloping sepals shelter the corolla from the rain. However, Lady Thumb is covered in such a mass of flowers that, no matter the slight fault, it is a must for growing outdoors. (1966, Roe)

*Lena Dalton Double. Tube pale pink; sepals recurved, pale pink; corolla blue, ageing to rose-mauve. Flowers medium sized and freely produced amongst small, darkish-green foliage. Growth upright and bushy. (1953, Reimers)

Leonora Single. Tube, sepals and corolla soft pink. Medium-sized, bell-shaped flowers, on a plant of upright, vigorous habit. Needs to be in its second or third year before becoming a show stopper. (1960, Tiret)

Liebriez Semi-double. Tube and sepals pale cerise; corolla pinkish white veined red. Growth upright and bushy. A small-flowered, small-leaved, free-flowering cultivar ideal for small pot work. It is also very hardy and can be used in a permanent planting feature with any of the Thumb family. It does not like growing in a greenhouse so keep it outside. (1874, Kohene)

*Linda Goulding Single. Tube short, white; sepals reflexed, pink; corolla white, veined with pink. Stamens and pistil bright red. Bell-shaped, medium-sized flowers. Foliage green on a self-branching plant of upright habit. Ideal for small pot culture. (1981, Goulding)

*Lindisfarne Semi-double. Tube short, thick, pale pink; sepals pale pink with darker flush towards the edges; corolla dark violet. Very short jointed. A vigorous grower with a self-branching habit. An excellent hanging pot plant. (1974, Ryle-Atkinson)

*Little Beauty Single. Tube and sepals flesh-pink; corolla lavender-blue. Very free flowering with small blossoms and a compact, bushy habit. Recommended for small pot cultivation. Raiser and date of introduction unknown.

*Lochinver Semi-double to double. Tube pale pink; sepals reflexed, pink; corolla purple shading to pink at the base. Filaments and style pink; stigma a creamy white. Medium-sized flowers amongst dark green, ovate foliage. Medium growth habit, self branching. Recommended for training as a bush or standard. (1983, Mitchinson)

*Loeky Single. Tube short, thick, rosy-red; sepals upturned, rosy-red; corolla lavender, ageing to rose-pink. Medium-sized flowers with conspicuous red stamens. Leaves light green. Growth upright and bushy. A good pot plant. (1981, de Graaff)

*Lord Roberts Single. Tube short, scarlet; sepals scarlet; corolla purplish-violet. Large flowers, very early and freely produced. Bushy upright growth. Makes a good pyramid. (1909, Lemoine)

Love's Reward Single. Tube and sepals pale rose-pink; corolla pale pink. Growth is short-jointed.

Lucky Strike Semi-double. Tube ivory-pink; sepals ivory-pink with darker reverses; corolla bluish-purple; outer petals pink with purple markings. Large flowers, freely produced. A good vigorous grower. (1943, Niederholzer)

This cultivar is always a winner in the Best Plant in Show class. Bred by the late Cliff Gadsby, Margaret Roe is a single cultivar which needs a little pinching but is very rewarding

Lyes Unique Single. Tube and sepals white; corolla salmon-orange. An old-fashioned, free-flowering kind that is well worth growing. Strong, bushy, upright growth. (1886, Lye)

Madame Cornelissen Semi-double. Scarlet-red tube and sepals; corolla white veined red; dark green leaves growing on strong bushy stems. Free flowering and absolutely hardy. Very good as a hedge some 90-120cm (3-4ft) high. One of the good older cultivars, very easy for the newcomer to grow — there are not many red and white hardies. (1860, Cornelissen)

*****Margaret** Semi-double. Tube and sepals carmine scarlet; medium-sized corolla violet veined red. A very strong grower, free flowering, upright and very hardy indeed. It has proved itself without doubt at Harlow Car as one of the best cultivars growing in the hardy trial beds. Suitable for the shrubbery border or as a hedge growing to 120cm (4ft) or more, with dark green foliage. (1937, Wood)

*****Margaret Pilkington** Single. Tube and sepals white with rose-bengal veining and patching. Corolla violet, ageing to purple. Free-flowering, medium-sized blossoms. Short jointed with a bushy upright habit. A good cultivar for a basket or hanging pot. (1984, Clark)

*****Margaret Roe** Single. Tube and sepals rosy-red; corolla pale violet-purple. Medium-sized blossoms, held upright. Upright, bushy growth. Almost hardy, and first class for bedding as well as bush and shrub culture. A good beginner's plant. (1968, Gadsby)

*****Marilyn** Double. Tube pink; sepals broad, pink; corolla white. A vigorous but lax grower of free-branching habit. Requires constant pinching back. (1961, Martin)

*****Marinka** Single. Tube and sepals rich red; corolla dark red. Very prolific. Medium-sized blossoms produced on strong, cascading growth. A first-class basket and hanging pot cultivar, which is well suited to training as a weeping standard. (1902, Rozain-Boucharlat)

Masquerade Double. Tube short, flesh-pink to pink; sepals flesh-pink to pink; corolla purple; outer petals marbled pink. Large blossoms on a free-flowering plant of trailing habit. (1963, Kennett)

*****Mickey Goult** Single. Tube short, white; sepals short, broad, white on top, pale pink beneath; corolla purple, paler towards the edge. Light green foliage on a bushy, upright plant. Can be kept very neat and compact by regular pinching. One of the finest cultivars for cultivation as a fan or espalier. (1981, Roe)

*****Mieke Meursing** Single to semi-double. Tube and sepals red; corolla pale pink with darker, prominent veining. Short jointed, bushy and extremely vigorous. Ideal for the beginner. (1968, Hopwood)

*****Minirose** Single. Tube long, pale rose; sepals pointed, pale rose, darker rose beneath; corolla dark rose with lighter veining. Very prolific, with a bushy upright habit. Short jointed and first class for small pot work or miniature standards. (1983, de Graaff)

*****Miss California** Semi-double. Tube short, pink; sepals long, pointed, pink; corolla white with pink flush inside and faint pink, basal veining. Flowers long, beautifully proportioned and produced on a neat plant of lax habit. A good plant in the second year. Recommended for basket work if weighted. (1950, Hodges)

*****Mission Bells** Single. Tube and sepals scarlet; corolla rich purple with cerise splashes near the base. Medium-sized, bell-shaped blossoms which sometimes throw semi-doubles. Upright, bushy growth, becoming leggy in the greenhouse. Best placed outside during the summer. (1948, Walker and Jones)

*Mrs Lovell Swisher   Single. Tube long, flesh-pink; sepals white, flushed with pink and with green tips, pink beneath; corolla rose. Small flowers produced early in the season and in abundance. Upright habit, vigorous. Can be used successfully for a standard, conical shape or pyramid. A good beginner's plant. (1942, Reeves)

*Mrs Marshall   Single. Tube and sepals creamy-white; corolla rose-cerise. Free flowering with medium-sized blossoms. Upright, bushy growth. Can be trained to almost any shape. (c1862, Jones) (AM, 1929)

*Nancy Lou   Double. Tube pale pink; sepals deep pink and reflexed; corolla white. Upright growth with large blossoms freely produced. Benefits from shading. (1971, Stubbs)

Natasha Sinton   Double. Tube orchid pink; sepals orchid pink tipped green; corolla orchid pink veined magenta. A beautiful new variety with classic blooms of medium to large size; colours variable in sun and shade. Easy to grow, it makes an excellent subject for a basket. (1990, R. Sinton)

*Nellie Nuttall   Single. Tube small, bright red; sepals small, deep crimson; corolla white with red veining. Pink filaments, bright red pistil. Very erect, small flowers produced in abundance. Self cleaning – that is the blossoms drop away cleanly as they expire. Light green, ovate foliage. A compact plant with neat, upright growth. Recommended for bush or shrub culture. (1977, Roe)

Nicholas Hughes   Single. Tube pink; sepals pink with a scarlet line running lengthwise down the centre culminating in green tips; corolla creamy-white with contrasting scarlet anthers. Produces more than one flower in each leaf axil. Dark green foliage with serrated leaf edges. An upright growing, self-branching fuchsia which will produce an exciting

Miss California. When grown with care and expertise this pink-and-white, semi-double trailing fuchsia takes some beating. One of the best to come out of the USA, it is well worth growing as a bush once it has made some hard wood. At two years old it can be used in a 15cm (6in) pot for show work

show plant. Certainly one for the beginner, as it forms a neat and tidy bush without much effort. (1982, Clark)

*Nimue Single. Tube short, pink; sepals pale flesh-pink to cream, pink undersides, recurved; corolla pink to mauve, each petal having a dark blue edge. Small flowers produced freely on a bushy, upright, short-jointed plant with pleasing, light green foliage. Makes a good, compact pot plant. (1983, Goulding)

Orange Drops Single. Almost self deep orange flower, with a slightly deeper shade of orange in the corolla. Flowers hang more in clusters than in separate leaf axils along the length of the stem. Orange cultivars tend to be of soft growth and rather lax in habit, and it is a colour which is not at its best indoors. Leaves on the large side and are an initial source of botrytis setting in. Much admired, but difficult to grow well. (1963, Martin)

*Orange Flare Single. Tube short, thick, salmon-orange; sepals short and thick, salmon-orange; corolla orange shading to pale orange at base. Early and free flowering with medium-sized blossoms. Needs to be grown with good light in order to develop a strong colour. Growth habit upright, bushy and self-branching. Requires little pinching. (1972, Handley)

*Other Fellow Single. Tube white; sepals white tipped green; corolla coral-pink with white base. Rather small flowers, but produced in abundance. Upright bushy growth. (1946, Hazard and Hazard)

*Pacquesa Single. Tube short, deep red; sepals reflexed, deep red; corolla white with red veining. Large flowers, freely produced amongst bright green leaves. Upright, short-jointed and bushy habit. (1974, Clyne)

*Papoose Semi-double. Tube and sepals scarlet; co-

rolla deep purple. Flowers on the small side, but produced en masse; leaves small and dark green; very hardy, though a little ragged in shape. One for the rockery, but not for the greenhouse or show-bench. Can be trained to almost any shape. A dominant hardy fuchsia in the beds at Harlow Car. (1980, Reedstrom)

Party Frock Single to semi-double. Tube long, rose-pink; sepals upturned, rose-pink tipped with green; corolla blue splashed with pink. Flowers large on an upright, bushy plant. Should be pinched early. (1953, Walker and Jones)

Patio Princess Double. Tube and sepals cardinal red; corolla white veined pink. Short-jointed and florif-erous, this is one for the show bench. (1988, R. Sinton)

*****Pennine** Single. Tube carmine striped with red; sepals white with red base; corolla deep violet-blue fading towards the base. Medium-sized flowers on an upright, bushy plant. Makes a marvellous standard and a super basket when weights are used. (1979, Hitchinson)

*****Perry Park** Single. Tube short, thick, pale pink; sepals reflexed, deep pink, paler inside; corolla bright rose fading towards the base. Medium-sized blossoms with up to six individuals at each leaf joint. Upright, short-jointed growth. Makes a good standard and is well suited to bedding. (1977, Handley)

Phyllis Semi-double. Tube and sepals rose red; corolla rosy cerise. A small flower, produced in large numbers to cover the plant, but blooms do produce more than the required four sepals. This was origi-nally a fault on the show bench, but BFS rules have been relaxed on this point (see Chapter 8) and extra sepals shall not now be counted as a cultural fault (in our opinion, a backward step). In the greenhouse Phyllis can get out of hand, as it grows very quickly

*Other Fellow, another
cultivar from the USA,
produces a profusion of
small, near-perfect
blooms*

and strongly. Hardy, and should be grown outside as either a bush, standard or pyramid. An ideal plant for the patio, grown in a tub or large pot as a standard. Also ideal for use when a hedge is required, growing to just over 120cm (4ft). (1938, Brown)

Pink Bon Accorde Single. Almost self pink : tube and sepals pale pink, sepals deeper pink underneath and tipped green; deeper shaded pink corolla is a shade paler at the base. Flowers plentiful, but smaller in size. Leaves also small sized, and medium green. An upright growing bush which needs a little extra pinching out for a good shape. (1959, Thorne)

Pink Fantasia Double. Tube rose, fading to white; sepals pale pink; corolla light purple. A good, upright growing show plant. (P.Webb)

Pink Galore Double. Tube and sepals (which curl upwards to the tube) a deeper pink in colour than the corolla, which is nearer candy pink. Shiny dark green leaves. A trailing cultivar best grown in a hanging pot or as one variety in a mixed hanging container. Can make a good half basket, but not of good enough growth to fill a full basket. With experience, can be grown as a weeping standard. Prone to botrytis in its early stages and must be kept on the dry side. To obtain the best colour it should be allowed to flower in the greenhouse in shade, or under a sheltered patio where it will have protection. One which is sold in great numbers, but beginners can easily be disappointed for it presents a real test of growing skills. (1958, Fuchsia-La)

*Pink Pearl Semi-double. Tube pale pink; sepals incurved, pale pink; corolla pink, lightly flushed with rose. Medium-sized blossoms that are sometimes fully double. Bushy, upright growth. First class for pyramids, conical shapes and pillars. Makes a good standard too. (1919, Bright)

*Pink Quartet Semi-double. Tube deep pink; sepals upturned, deep pink; corolla pale pink. Large flowered with upright, bushy growth. Excellent for a standard. (1949, Walker and Jones)

*Plenty Single. Tube thick, carmine; sepals rose, pale beneath; corolla violet-purple veined with carmine. A profusely flowered cultivar with an abundance of small to medium blossoms. Short-jointed, bushy and of upright habit. Suited to all forms of training, except basket work. (1974, Gadsby)

*Pop Whitlock Single. Tube and sepals pale pink; corolla violet. Very short, medium-sized flowers. A handsome, variegated-foliage cultivar of somewhat lax growth. Leaves light greyish-green with a creamy-white edge. It is for this characteristic that it is almost exclusively grown, being well suited to life in a hanging basket. (1984, Head)

President Leo Boullemier Single. The parents of this cultivar being Joy Patmore and Cloverdale Pearl should produce a top class fuchsia and indeed they did so. Short tube streaked magenta; sepals white and held out at an angle, flared well away from the tube. Perfectly bell-shaped corolla, magenta-blue fading to blush pink with age. Dark green foliage a little on the large side, with a prominent serrated edge. Growth upright, short-jointed and bushy. Grown with very little heat it will produce a neat, tight bush. One for the show bench, and ideal for the beginner. Named after a former President of the British Fuchsia Society, it is a top class plant. (1983, Burns)

*President Margaret Slater Single. Tube thin, white; sepals long, white flushed with pink and tipped green, salmon-pink beneath; corolla mauve-pink overlaid with salmon. Flowers medium sized and freely produced. Foliage dark green with conspicuous red veining. Naturally produces trailing growths, but apart from its obvious use for basket work it can be thoroughly recommended for espaliers, fans and standards. (1972, Taylor)

*Prosperity Double. Thick crimson tube; sepals firm and waxy; corolla pale neyron rose, flushed and veined rosy red. Produces a large number of blooms of medium size. Dark green, glossy foliage, on the large side and mainly formed as three leaves at each leaf joint. Growth upright and bushy, and at its best as a hardy in the garden border. Easy but satisfying. (1970, Gadsby)

Quaser Double. Trailing type growth which is what they excel in. Tube and sepals white; corolla dauphine violet with mixture of white at the base. Although large it produces plenty of blooms, at their best colour in shade. Trailing type American cultivars, for use in a hanging basket of mixed flowers. Not always easy. (1974, Walker)

*Rebecca Williamson Double. Tube peach; sepals pink with orange-rose undersides; corolla pink; outer petals striped deep peach and salmon. Strong growing, but somewhat lax habit. (1986, Redfern)

Red Spider Single. Tube long, deep crimson; sepals narrow, recurving deep crimson; corolla deep rose, veined and margined crimson. Medium-sized flowers on vigorous, trailing shoots. A good basket plant. (1946, Reiter)

*Reg Dickenson Single. Tube short, pink; sepals long, narrow, pink with green tips; corolla purple. Leaves mid-green, serrated, on a plant of spreading, bushy habit. A good bush or basket cultivar. (1985)

Robbie Single. Short pale magenta tube; sepals held out horizontally, pale magenta on top fading to white with green tips, recurving; corolla white with very little veining. Flowers medium sized and flared like a coolie hat when fully open – a well grown plant is a sight to behold. Leaves medium green on a tidy, upright, bushy plant. Needs that extra bit of care and attention, and a little extra pinching out. Recommended for the beginner nevertheless. A real show stopper. (1984, Lamb)

*Rosecroft Beauty Semi-double. Tube short, thick, carmine-red; sepals carmine tipped with green; corolla white, flushed and veined with carmine. Small flowers amongst pale green leaves edged with gold, cream and cerise. A fickle cultivar worth trying if you can get it. (1968, Eden)

Rose of Castile Single. Waxy white tube and sepals faintly flushed pink, sepals tipped green; purple corolla flushed rose, with a whitish bottom. Hardy, but very free flowering, with small to medium flowers. Upright and bushy growing, and a must in the garden for its unusual colouring. Will make a strong-growing standard, and a good pot plant can be formed with pinching. (1855, Bank)

*Roy Walker Double. Tube white, flushed with pink; sepals reflexed, white, tinged with pink; corolla white. Free flowering, with small blossoms borne amongst upright, bushy growth. Medium-sized, green leaves, slightly serrated. An American introduction that enjoys the warm conditions that can lead to botrytis. (1975, Walker)

*Royal Purple Semi-double. Tube short, broad, deep cerise; sepals upturned, cerise; corolla purple, fading towards the base. Large flowered, prolific and early. Bushy upright growth which renders it suitable for training as a bush – better after two or three years, standard or pyramid. (1896, Lemoine)

Royal Velvet Double. Tube and sepals crimson red, sepals upturned and curling back towards the tube; very large corolla a deep rich purple with crimson splashes. As the flower fades it turns to red, giving a contrast between the two colours on the plant at the same time. Growth very vigorous; although upright it tends to arch over, the size of the flowers pulling the branches down. A good choice for novices in the doubles class with its large flowers and excellent colour, though flowering is not profuse. Medium green leaves not as large as one would

expect. Can be trained as a standard. (1962, Waltz)

*Rufus** Single. All red self – a lovely turkey-red in colour. Always in bloom, flowers plentiful. Leaves medium green. Very easy to grow as a pot plant or garden hardy. Recommended for beginners.

*Sandboy** Single. Tube short, thin, pink; sepals narrow, curled, deep pink; corolla deep mauve, paler

Roy Walker is a superb double white cultivar. Though not the easiest fuchsia to grow, it will repay every effort

towards the base. Small flowers borne in profusion. Upright, short-jointed plant of bushy habit. Perfect for the home. (1967, Hall-Atkinson)

Santa Cruz Semi-double to double. Tube and sepals deep crimson; corolla dark crimson. Large blooms carried amongst lush green foliage with red veining. A good, bushy plant for training into a standard. A first-class plant for the cut-bloom classes. (1947, Tiret)

Shelford Single. Tube light rose; sepals baby pink; corolla white. Very floriferous and has already won many top awards. (1986)

*Siobhan Semi-double. Tube rose; sepals white, rose shading towards base, rose beneath; corolla white, tinged with pink towards the base. Pistil long and pink. Medium-sized blossoms with attractively curled petals. Growth upright and bushy. (1976, Rye)

*Snowcap Semi-double. Tube and sepals bright red; corolla white, slight cerise veining. By modern standards quite small blossoms, but produced in abundance. Amongst the best of the old-style cultivars. Growth vigorous and upright. Can be strongly recommended for training as a pyramid, conical shape or pillar and makes a commendable standard too. (*c*1880, Henderson)

*Strawberry Delight Double. Tube and sepals crimson; corolla white with petaloids heavily flushed with carmine-rose. Large to medium blossoms produced amongst most interesting foliage that starts off yellowish-green and bronze, but turns green with maturity. Upright habit, excellent for bedding. (1969, Gadsby)

*String of Pearls Single to semi-double. Tube pale rose; sepals paler rose; corolla rose-purple with lavender veins. A very prolific, free-flowering cultivar with very uniformly shaped blossoms. Growth strong with an upright habit. (1976, Pacey)

*Sunray Single. Tube and sepals cerise; corolla rose-purple. The flowers are relatively small and not the main feature of this lovely foliage cultivar. Leaves are pale green edged with creamy-white and flushed with red. To maintain such handsomely coloured foliage this cultivar needs restricting to a small pot and providing with well-lit conditions. It makes a good bedding subject or pot plant. Exact origin unclear – an old cultivar from the last century. (AM, 1929)

Superstar Single. Tube pale pink; sepals white flushed pink; corolla pale amethyst violet fading to magenta. Flowers are medium-sized, held horizontally and produced in profusion. Growth is upright and self-branching. (1988, R. Sinton)

*Swanley Gem Single. Tube and sepals scarlet; corolla violet, fading at base and with scarlet veining. Upright, bushy growth supporting beautifully proportioned, medium-sized flowers in which the corolla flattens out like a saucer. An old, but reliable kind for the newcomer. (1901, Cannell)

*Swingtime Double. Tube short, red; sepals red; corolla white, veined with pink. Well-proportioned, dark green leaves are carried on red stems. An easy cultivar of upright, but somewhat lax growth which is adaptable to most forms of training. It makes an exceptional standard as well as a good basket plant. (1950, Tiret)

*Taddle Single. Tube short, deep rose-pink; sepals fully reflexed, deep rose-pink; corolla white, occasionally veined with pink. Stamens and pistil pink. Medium-sized flowers produced freely. A vigorous grower with light green foliage and an upright, bushy habit. (1974, Gubler)

*Task Force Single. Tube long, white; sepals white with lilac flush beneath; corolla cyclamen-purple

Waveney Waltz. The pink sepals and white corolla, together with its pale foliage and neat habit of growth, make this an ideal plant for the showman. Perhaps not one of the easiest, but certainly one with which to persevere

ageing to magenta. Magenta stamens with pale lilac anthers. Lilac stigma and style. Rather large vulgar green foliage on a strong, bushy, upright-growing plant. Requires frequent pinching and is at its best after two or three years' training. Makes a lovely standard. (1984, Redfern)

*Tennessee Waltz Semi-double to double. Tube rose-madder; sepals curved, rose-madder; corolla lilac splashed with rose. Filaments and style rose. A very easy, vigorous plant with medium-sized blossoms amongst fine, green foliage. The growth habit is bushy and upright. A good plant for the novice. Can easily be trained into a standard. (1951, Walker and Jones)

*Ting-a-Ling Single. Tube, sepals and corolla white.

Large flowers with bold, reflexed sepals and flared petals. Growth upright, bushy and relatively easy to train; unfortunately it suffers rather badly from botrytis. (1959, Schnabel-Paskesen)

*Tom Knights Single. Tube short, white to flesh pink; sepals white with pinkish cast, pink beneath; corolla lavender to violet, shading to white at base of petals. Medium-sized flowers are produced in abundance amongst light green, ovate leaves, so many that in its early days the plant will require staking in order to take their weight. Vigorous, upright growth, self-branching and short-jointed. Excellent for training. Produces a fine standard. (1983, Goulding)

*Upward Look Single. Tube short, carmine; sepals short, broad, carmine, tipped with green; corolla pale purple. Flowers short and held erect. A shade lover which has a bushy, upright habit. (1968, Gadsby)

*Vi Whitehouse Single. Tube greenish; sepals greenish-white with a hint of pink; corolla rose, veined with carmine. Compact, short-jointed bush. Seems to have great promise for the show bench. (1987)

Waveney Waltz Single. Tube short, pink; sepals pink; corolla white, lightly veined. Medium-sized flowers in profusion. Rather unfortunately it occasionally throws an extra petal. Bushy, upright growth with light green foliage. Ideal for bush or shrub culture. (1982, Burns)

*Westminster Chimes Semi-double. Tube deep rose; sepals rose, fading to pale pink, tipped with green; corolla violet-blue ageing to magenta. Flowers smallish, colouring better in sunshine. Rather lax growth with small or medium, bright green leaves. Highly recommended for shrub, bush, hanging pot and small pot culture. (1976, Clyne)

*White Joy Single. Tube short, white, tinged with pink; sepals broad white, tinged with pink; corolla white and taking the shape of a bell. Medium-sized flowers amongst handsome, green foliage produced from strong, upright, short-jointed growth. Can be grown as a standard as well as a bush or shrub and is highly recommended. (1980, Burns)

*Winston Churchill** Double. Tube long, pink; sepals broad and reflexed, pink, tipped with green; corolla lavender-blue, ageing to purple. Medium-sized blossoms produced in abundance. Upright, bushy habit. An easy cultivar, but sometimes temperamental in the winter. (1942, Garson)

The descriptions of cultivars given here are adequate for most practical gardeners. Detailed descriptions of these and many more cultivars are to be found in the standard *Checklist of Species, Hybrids and Cultivars of the Genus Fuchsia* (see Further Reading).

11
Pests and Diseases

It is easy to become depressed by pests and diseases, for there appear to be so many that can attack your plants, with devastating effect. In practice, although many will appear from time to time, it is not an impossible task to control them.

A spraying routine from bud break until leaf fall helps to provide a measure of protection, especially if you use systemic chemicals. These are absorbed by the plant system and provide protection from either sucking insects or fungal diseases for two or three weeks at a time.

By spraying regularly with an insecticide containing dimethoate and a fungicide in which the active ingredient is benomyl, a degree of protection can be afforded. It is true that some resistance to these chemicals can be built up by pests and pathogens, so it is perhaps prudent periodically to switch to another – take the advice of your local garden centre. Use contact killers such as malathion when you see the pest, for they have to come in direct contact with it for control to be effective.

The whole area of chemical control is fraught with difficulties for the uninitiated, so in order to keep abreast of latest developments take advantage of some of the excellent literature now supplied freely by chemical companies. With recent legislation regarding pesticide sales, storage and use, we can all become better informed much more easily.

*Colourful fuchsias
growing in the border,
backed by blowsy
double-flowered
begonias. Mixing
different plants together
can reduce the incidence
of pests and diseases*

PESTS

There are many more pests than those noted here that could attack your fuchsias, for many insects have wide-ranging appetites. Those described are the ones you are most likely to encounter.

Aphids

These are popularly known as greenfly or plant lice and come in pink, yellow or black as well as green. There are some five hundred species in Britain and Northern Europe, many with widely varying palates. None are specific to the genus *Fuchsia*, but many enjoy sucking the succulent foliage, causing distortion and disfigurement. Sooty mould is a secondary occurrence developing on the sticky honeydew exuded by the aphids. Non-chemical methods of control are, for the most part, ineffective. Spraying regularly with a systemic insecticide containing dimethoate should effect a control. A contact killer like malathion can be used when the aphids are present.

Capsid Bugs

There are several capsid bugs. They are usually green or brownish, small, hard bugs, which produce wingless nymphs. Both generations pierce plant tissue and cause distortion and tattering of foliage and flowers. Regularly spraying with a systemic insecticide containing dimethoate or formitrothion provides a measure of control, as does the use of contact killers such as malathion and fenitrothion when the pests are seen. Garden and greenhouse hygiene make the most significant contribution to their control, for they hide and overwinter in fallen plant debris.

Caterpillars

Theoretically any number of caterpillars could attack your fuchsias, but in practice it is likely to be either the angle shades moth or the carnation tortrix moth. It matters little which species it is, for the most successful way of dealing with such a problem in fuchsias is likely to be hand control, that is, picking off the caterpillars by hand. If you must resort to chemical means, then non-persistent contact insecticides such as derris and malathion can be used. Some growers prefer more persistent insecticides such as those containing permethrin.

Glasshouse Red Spider Mites

This is very troublesome if the atmosphere in the greenhouse is not damp enough. Red spiders dislike damp, and a regularly damped-down greenhouse will

---

DIAGNOSING PROBLEMS

All the following pests and diseases are likely to be found at some time on your fuchsias unless a rigorous spraying regime is implemented. Even then, there is no guarantee that your stock will remain untroubled.

Symptoms	Pest or Disease
Small greyish-white winged insects and yellow scales on undersides of leaves. Foliage often sticky and sooty.	Glasshouse whitefly
Green, yellow or pink winged or wingless small insects on shoots and leaves. Foliage sticky and sooty.	Aphids
Leaves dappled and stippled with yellow or bronze, and slowly dying and dropping off. Tiny mites on the undersides of foliage.	Glasshouse red spider mites
Small ragged holes in leaves and at tips of young shoots.	Capsid bugs
Plants collapse and small white grubs are seen in the compost feeding on the roots.	Vine weevil

Symptoms	Pest or Disease
Plants smothered with small, narrow-bodied, yellow, brown or black, winged or wingless insects. Shoots and flower buds damaged both indoors and out.	Thrips
Irregular holes chewed out of leaves, and young shoots damaged.	Caterpillars
Leaves wilt, inside of stem has black or brown streaking.	Wilt
Leaves with pale yellow patches and rusty-looking areas underneath.	Rust
Damping off and brown-leaf rots which spread to the stem.	**Botrytis
Fluffy, grey, fungal mould on stems, flowers or leaves.	**Grey mould

**Botrytis symptoms, as recognised by gardeners, are caused by the same pathogen, *Botrytis cinerea*, as the one which causes the disease we call grey mould.

rarely have a serious problem. Glasshouse red spider mite clings beneath the leaves of plants in a very fine 'web', feeding on plant tissue and causing mottling, and ultimately the death of, the leaves. Misting plants with clear water a couple of times a day will prevent the mites from becoming established, but if you have an infestation, then try to effect some control with contact killers like derris and malathion. Neither of these chemicals, nor indeed any others in the gardeners armoury, are reliably effective against this pest. Good hygiene and high moisture levels are the best preventatives.

Glasshouse Whitefly

This is the bane of the fuchsia grower. A constant battle is waged to control this pest which can be so easily brought in on a cutting or purchased plant. Symptoms of general debilitation in the plant are associated with clouds of small insects which all leap into the air like a miniature snowstorm when an infested plant is touched. Greenhouse hygiene helps in their control, but the most important thing to do is to keep hitting the pests at weekly intervals with a varying array of chemicals. Try malathion, pyrethrum and permethrin as contact killers and use these in conjunction with systemic insecticides containing dimethoate and formitrothion. If you appear to have a buildup of resistance in the whitefly, as is happening in the south of Britain, then use derris and resmethrin to try to overcome it. HCH and dichlorvos fumigants can be used effectively against adult whiteflies.

Thrips

Severe infestations of these on plants in a glasshouse are largely the result of poor cultural conditions: too much warmth and too little water. A cool, humid atmosphere helps to prevent their occurrence and proliferation. Spray infested plants with malathion at two to three weekly intervals.

Vine Weevil

This is a serious pest of a wide range of greenhouse plants. It is not until the plant has wilted and is on the point of collapse that you know that anything is wrong. The white grubs of this inconspicuous brown weevil live in the soil or compost and eat the roots of plants until virtually nothing remains. Good hygiene helps to control its occurrence, but much can be done to dissuade its appearance by mixing HCH dust into the potting compost at potting time. Dousing plants that are vulnerable with a systemic insecticide, so that when the grubs start eating the plant they imbibe the poison, also helps. If you detect vine weevil, then it is a wise precaution to repot all vulnerable plants, breaking open the rootballs and inspecting for grubs. This cannot always be done with show or specimen plants when they are in the middle of their growing cycle, but young plants will come to no serious harm if disturbed.

DISEASES

While it is possible for fuchsias to be afflicted by a wide range of diseases, few regularly appear. With the exception of rust, which is scarce in this country anyway, a measure of protection can be afforded by using at regular intervals a systemic fungicide containing benomyl.

Botrytis/Grey Mould

These two maladies, caused by the same pathogen, *Botrytis cinerea*, manifest themselves in different ways, but both can be controlled by the regular use of benomyl. Too damp an atmosphere, often with the plants under stress, leads to this disease taking a hold. Adequate ventilation, good greenhouse hygiene and cultural practice should help to keep the problem at bay. It has to be accepted that some cultivars are more prone to botrytis than others, so if your conditions are conducive to its appearance seek to avoid susceptible plants.

Gold Runner. This exciting golden-variegated fuchsia is of quite recent introduction and is very floriferous. It is also resistant to botrytis

Rust

This is very unusual in Britain, but as its alternative host is willow herb, it should be watched for at all times. Any plants that are affected should be burnt; alternatively, strip off all leaves and 'skeletonise' the plant.

Wilt

Wilts usually result from disruption or blockage in the water-conducting tissue in the stem, resulting from the

---

ORGANIC CHEMICALS

More and more gardeners are turning to organic gardening, which means that they do not use inorganic chemical fertilisers or chemical sprays. If used properly according to instructions and with the care they demand, then we personally believe that chemical sprays are the first line of defence. However, there are a limited number of 'organic' pesticides in use, although not all are available to the amateur.

Derris This is a substance made from members of the chrysanthemum family. It is a safe insecticide for use against many pests including aphids, caterpillars and red spider mite.

Pyrethrum Care must be taken with this substance as it is highly poisonous. It is used against attacks of aphids and leafhoppers, but it will also kill bees.

Nicotine Although no longer available to the amateur gardener, nicotine shreds have been replaced in use by a liquid formulation of nicotine. This is very effective against attacks of aphids and thrips. Nicotine is the most powerful and most poisonous of these 'organic' substances, and will obviously kill bees and some bird life.

Insecticidal Soaps These are made from naturally fatty acids and are harmless to humans, birds and bees.

---

production of toxins by a group of pathogens of the groups *Verticillium* and *Fusarium*. Such fungal assailants enjoy cold, damp, clammy conditions. They frequently affect plants growing in compost that is too wet, and are also often associated with overpotting – the provision of too large a pot too soon. Dirty pots help the spread of wilt, so potting-shed hygiene is vital. There is no reliable cure, although it is always worth drenching the compost with benomyl. Infected plants are best destroyed. Unfortunately the disease has usually gone too far before you notice it.

The exciting news is that the Phostrogen company has introduced a range of non-toxic, natural/organic pesticides from Ontario in Canada. They are on sale to the amateur, in ready-to-use spray bottles. The products will be soap based, and could revolutionise our use of the current harmful chemical sprays.

One of the old fashioned methods of dealing with plants infected with whitefly was to wash the leaves between finger and thumb with soapy water. This proved effective, particularly if the eggs were washed off as well, but as only the leaves were washed, and often many were missed, eggs were left on them and the stems and the breeding cycle continued. This new Phostrogen product must be given a full test by everyone if we are to reduce the use of chemical insecticides and pesticides.

However, a very safe alternative to this is the use of Phostrogen pesticide sticks, which are inserted into the compost. The chemical is absorbed by the roots of the plant and is drawn upwards through the stem to the branches and leaves, thus producing a systemic effect throughout the plant. This ensures that anything which nibbles at growth above compost level will take up the chemical and die. The substances also remain inside the plant for a period of time, and so besides killing the adult pests, the newly-hatched youngsters will also die.

12
The Fuchsia Grower's Calendar

Fuchsia growing is a year-round occupation. It has its peaks and troughs, but scarcely a week passes by without the need to undertake some small task. This applies to the indoor hobby gardener as well as the serious exhibitor; only outdoor growers are spared activity during the winter months and even they need to keep an eye on their charges then.

This calendar is arranged with weeks 1-5 being midway through the winter period (Jan/Feb), the start of the season.

WEEKS 1-5

Check plants in store and see that they are only slightly moist.

Any plants which you have doubts about should be discarded.

In the Heated Greenhouse

If you have a propagator, utilise it for cuttings taken from older plants when you pinch them out.

Ensure that the atmosphere in the greenhouse remains dry and not too warm. The plants should be kept damp.

Feed mature plants with your usual liquid feed diluted to about a quarter strength.

Ventilate for at least half an hour each day when weather permits.

Ensure that you have adequate stand-by heating arrangements in case of an emergency.

Look through the newly arrived catalogues and order your new season's rooted cuttings now.

Turn plants regularly so that they receive an even amount of light.

WEEKS 6-10

Make a final check on plants that are being overwintered indoors.

If you have a heated greenhouse, move some of the plants there and spray lightly each day with tepid water to soften the bark.

In the Heated Greenhouse

Continue to take cuttings. Those rooted last month can be potted and weaned to the cooler conditions of the open greenhouse.

A good bush of the extremely free flowering double cultivar Prosperity, which is possibly at its best when grown as a garden hardy. A must for the keen gardener – there is a definite shortage of double hardy fuchsias – Prosperity also makes a good standard for use on the show bench

Start the spraying routine, using both a systemic insecticide and a fungicide. This must be continued regularly throughout the growing season.

Ventilate well whenever the weather permits.

Beware of clear skies and sunny days. They can do untold damage in an unventilated and unshaded greenhouse, causing scorching and uncharacteristic growth.

Previously ordered rooted cuttings for plants required for early shows during July and early August should arrive this month.

Hardy varieties should be growing away strongly now if they are to make substantial plants for planting out during June.

WEEKS 11-14

It is time to bring out plants which have been overwintering indoors, but do not risk them in an unheated greenhouse just yet. If you do not have a greenhouse, stand them in a cool place in the house.

In the Heated Greenhouse

Take cuttings if you have not already done so.

Repot any plants that were brought in last month.

Repot plants which have been grown on the biennial method (see section on overwintering in Chapter 4) as required.

Plant up hanging baskets to give them sufficient time to mature. This is essential for those being grown for showing.

Slightly increase the water supply for all plants.

Give a first foliar feed to plants that are growing strongly and continue feeding regularly until late summer.

Lightly spray older plants with clear tepid water.

Pinch out any plants that require shaping.

Continue to turn the plants on a regular basis so that all sides of the foliage receive equal amounts of light and a balanced plant is produced.

Increase the period of ventilation as the days lengthen

and the weather warms up.

An insecticidal strip can be hung up in the greenhouse. This will need replacement every month or so.

Keep compost for potting in the warmth of the greenhouse. The same applies to water which should, ideally, be at greenhouse temperature when used.

Shading should be provided towards the end of this period.

WEEKS 15-19

The show schedules should come to hand about now. Make a plan of just how many plants you require and, more especially, the pot sizes needed. Always plan to grow additional plants in case of emergency.

In the Greenhouse

Keep some newspaper handy to cover tender young plants if the weather turns cold, especially in the unheated greenhouse.

Take cuttings from biennial exhibition plants.

Towards the end of the month put larger plants outside during the day.

Also make use of a cold frame to begin the hardening-off process.

Make the final pinch this month for double-flowered cultivars required for show work.

Never work forward to a show date. Always get the date fixed and work back to the final pinch date according to the cultivars being grown.

Ventilate freely.

In the Garden

When you see the new shoots appearing above soil level on hardy cultivars, cut all last season's growth down almost to ground level, except on plants grown as a hedge.

Prick over the soil between the plants with a fork. Add a handful of bonemeal, sprinkling it around each plant and working it into the soil.

WEEKS 20-23
Place as many plants outside as possible to relieve the pressure on the overburdened greenhouse.

In the Greenhouse
Shade the greenhouse from scorching sun, but try to retain as much light as possible.
Implement a full and regular feeding programme.
Maintain the insecticidal and fungicidal spraying programme.
Pinch out both double and single cultivars intended for exhibition work. Remember that the final pinch is six to eight weeks beforehand for singles and ten to twelve weeks beforehand for doubles.
This is the ideal time to take cuttings for plants that are to be grown by the biennial method.
All final potting should be done now, especially of plants for showing.
Never pot on exhibition plants after the final pinch or you will disrupt timing.
Ventilate freely.

In the Garden
Spray hardy fuchsias with both a systemic insecticide and fungicide and continue regularly throughout the summer.
Sprinkle a little balanced fertiliser around established plants if you think it necessary.
Continue to harden off pot-grown plants required for the garden.
If frost threatens, bring susceptible plants indoors at night.

WEEKS 24-28
A time of rapid growth and development together with the arrival of insect pests and diseases.

In the Greenhouse
Make sure that the plants are not overcrowded and

Baskets of fuchsias positioned at eye level or just above enable the blooms to be seen at their very best. Used in conjunction with other summer basket plants, as in this Surrey garden, and placed in strategic positions, they are a real eyecatcher

that air can circulate freely around them.

Shading now needs to be increased.

Spray and damp the greenhouse down regularly with water.

Prepare to change the feed of exhibition plants from one of high nitrogen to a balanced or high-potash one.

Pot on young cuttings and place them outside in a shaded cold frame.

Pinch the growing points out of young cuttings as they attain an appropriate size.

In the Garden

Plant out hardy cultivars when all danger of frost has passed. (The second week in June is soon enough in the north.)

Put pot-grown plants out on their summer standing ground.

Hang baskets outside.

Plant standards out and provide them with good support.

Maintain a full pest and disease control programme.

Outdoor plants will benefit from a regular foliar feed now.

WEEKS 29-32

The start of the show season. Get show schedules out and check the dates for the closing of entries for the early shows.

In the Greenhouse

Ventilate freely.

Keep containers of water standing in the greenhouse to help maintain a moist atmosphere.

Use a high-potash feed on heavily budded flowering plants.

Give exhibition plants a foliar spray of Epsom salts before they come into bloom.

Ensure that plants which you are going to show have no sign of pests or disease. Use a greenhouse fumigating smoke where necessary rather than a heavy spray.

If there is a danger of bees damaging blossoms on show plants, cover all ventilators and doors to keep them out.

Make sure that all transportation material for the show is to hand (old net curtains, boxes, pot holders, etc). Make up an emergency box of spare clean pots, pencil, labels, string, stakes, scissors, name cards and some fresh peat.

In the Garden

The first flowers of the hardy varieties should appear during this period.

Check the staking of all plants outdoors, especially standards in the bedding scheme.

Inspect regularly for pests and diseases and maintain a regular spraying programme.

Make sure that baskets are kept well fed and watered and that they do not become waterlogged.

Give plants a high-potash feed and work it into the soil.

WEEKS 33-36

This is the peak time for fuchsia shows. Go to them and gather as much information as you can. Take a pen and paper with you and write down the names of any new cultivars which take your fancy.

In the Greenhouse

Mark the plants which you wish to keep for next year. Towards the end of this period remove the shading. Pot on young plants as and when necessary, pinching out when appropriate.

Ease up on the watering towards the end of this period. If show plants are slow to flower, spray with saltpetre seven to ten days before a show.

In the Garden

Feed with a high-potash fertiliser. Not only does this help with flowering, but it also assists with the ripening of wood in preparation for the winter.

Maintain the pest and disease spraying programme.
Lightly hoe the soil to control weeds and break up any surface capping.
Towards the end of this period, greenhouse-grown plants that are to be overwintered should be placed outside in order to ripen up the wood before the winter.

WEEKS 37-40

While the fuchsia flower display can last throughout this period, it is also a time of preparation for their winter vigil.

In the Greenhouse

Pot on any plants that are going to be kept growing through the winter.
Before bringing plants in from the garden, spray them thoroughly to ensure that they are free from pests and diseases.
Reduce watering now of plants that are to be cut back (see section on overwintering in Chapter 4) for the winter.
Remove any containers with water in them.

In the Garden

Make a final spray with insecticide and fungicide.
A final potash feed can be given during the early part of this period.

WEEKS 41-44

Be prepared for the first really damaging frosts about now.

In the Greenhouse

Water sparingly.
Inspect plants closely and keep all branches free from decaying leaves.
Colder nights will lead to condensation, so ventilate freely whenever possible.

Make sure that any plants which are due to be cut back are dried off sufficiently to prevent bleeding.

Continue to maintain a pest and disease control routine, but use smokes rather than sprays whenever possible.

In the Garden
Leave mature plants outside to catch the first two or three frosts. Take them in once the foliage is limp and ready to drop.

Take hanging baskets in.

Dig up standards before the first sharp frost. Lifting is a good form of root pruning. Place in pots, add a little peat or compost, and take indoors.

All except the hardy kinds should be put inside now.

WEEKS 45-49
The days are getting very short, often cold and sometimes damp and foggy too.

In the Heated Greenhouse
Provide insulation and maintain a low, but frost-free temperature.

Do everything possible to keep stale air moving on damp foggy days. A fan heater on low heat is ideal.

All plants that are to rest during the winter should be moved to their overwintering quarters.

In the Garden
Heap ashes or peat over the crowns of hardy cultivars. Do not cut them back.

WEEKS 50-52
Clean up tools and equipment, especially pots and labels, in preparation for the new season.

Appendices

Appendix 1: *Classification of Fuchsias*

Appendix 2: *Botanical Terms and Glossary*

Appendix 1

CLASSIFICATION OF FUCHSIAS

The genus *Fuchsia* belongs to the family *Onagraceae,* an interesting group of plants which embraces some twenty-one genera as diverse as evening primroses *(Oenothera)* and the willow herbs *(Epilobium)*. There are around one hundred species of fuchsia which are divided into seven distinct sections, although recent work suggests that there may only be ninety-seven, but as many as nine sections.

The following classification of *Fuchsia* is based upon that of Dr Philip Munz, Professor of Botany at Pomona College, California, USA, in his revision of the genus (1943). Despite amendments made later, this is still the standard work and the one upon which most botanists and gardeners rely. Under the classification of Munz the genus comprises around one hundred distinct species and is divided into seven sections.

SECTION 1: *Quelusia*. Flowers axillary, with the tube usually no longer than the sepals. Stamens long, exserted, leaves small.

SECTION 2: *Eufuchsia* (now often referred to as *Fuchsia)*. Flowers axillary, in terminal racemes or panicles. The tube is usually several times as long as the sepals. Stamens scarcely extended beyond the sepals. Leaves large opposite or whorled. Mostly free fruiting.

SECTION 3: *Kierschlegeria*. Flowers small, axillary. Petals almost as long, or the same length as the sepals, which are reflexed. Leaves with a thickened, persistent petiole base.

SECTION 4: *Skinnera*. Flowers very small, produced in clusters on old wood or above leaf axils on green shoots. Tube funnel-shaped. Petals small or lacking, sepals reflexed. Leaves small to medium sized arranged in an alternate fashion.

SECTION 5: *Hemsleyella*. Flowers axillary, in terminal racemes or panicles. Sepals much shorter than the tube, often joining at the base, petals lacking. Foliage medium sized.

SECTION 6: *Schufia*. Flowers borne in erect terminal panicles, nectary fused with the base of the tube. Leaves large.

SECTION 7: *Encliandra*. Flowers axillary, small, stamens short. Filaments reflex back into the tube. Leaves small.

SECTION 1: *Quelusia*

F. bracelinae	F. magellanica
F. campos-portoi	F. regia
F. coccinea	F. hybrida*

*Not strictly a species, but a naturally occurring hybrid allegedly of *F. magellanica* x *F. fulgens*.

SECTION 2: *Eufuchsia*

F. abrupta	F. confertifolia
F. andrei	F. cordifolia
F. asperifolia	F. corymbiflora
F. aspiazui	F. cuatrecasasii
F. asplundii	F. decussata
F. austromontana	F. denticulata
F. ayavacensis	F. fischeri
F. boliviana	F. fulgens
F. canescens	F. furfuracea

F. gehrigeri
F. glaberrima
F. hartwegii
F. hirtella
F. hypoleuca
F. jahnii
F. killipii
F. lehmanii
F. leptopoda
F. llewelynii
F. loxensis
F. macrophylla
F. macrostigma
F. magdalenae
F. mathewsii
F. munzii
F. osgoodii
F. ovalis
F. pallescens
F. petiolaris

F. pilosa
F. platypetola
F. polyantha
F. pringsheimii
F. putumayensis
F. rivularis
F. scabriuscula
F. sanctae-rosae
F. sessilifolia
F. simplicicaulis
F. smithii
F. splendens
F. storkii
F. sylvatica
F. tincta
F. townsendii
F. triphylla
F. venusta
F. verrucosa
F. woytkowskii

SECTION 3: *Kierschlegeria*
F. lycioides

SECTION 4: *Skinnera*
F. colensoi
F. cyrtandroides
F. excorticata

F. kirkii
F. perscandens
F. procumbens

SECTION 5: *Hemsleyella*
F. apetala
F. cestroides
F. decidua
F. garleppiana
F. hirsuta
F. juntasensis

F. macrantha
F. membranacea
F. salicifolia
F. tuberosa
F. tunariensis
F. unduavensis

SECTION 6: *Schufia*
F. arborescens

SECTION 7: *Encliandra*

F. *bacillaris*

F. *colimae*

F. *cylindracea*

F. *encliandra*

F. *hemsleyana*

F. *mexiae*

F. *michoacanensis*

F. *microphylla*

F. *minimifolia*

F. *minutifolia*

F. *pringlei*

F. *skutchiana*

F. *striolata*

F. *tacanensis*

F. *tetradactyla*

F. *thymifolia*

CULTIVATED FUCHSIAS

There are innumerable hybrids and cultivars of *Fuchsia*. Those in cultivation today are mostly the results of various unions between the following species: F. *magellanica,* F. *coccinea* and F. *fulgens,* with the undoubted influence of F. *boliviana* and F. *denticulata.* Characteristics of certain species are still clearly identifiable in their progeny and form distinct groups – F. *triphylla* for example.

Appendix 2

BOTANICAL TERMS AND GLOSSARY

Although botanical terms may seem alien it is important to be aware of them, for this is the common language of the fuchsia grower and commercial catalogue.

If we look at a fuchsia plant and disregard any particular method by which it is trained (shapes and habits are fully described when discussing training and showing in Chapters 5 and 7), it has several regular characteristics. Firstly, it has a **leading** or main growth with a **terminal shoot.** If the terminal shoot has been removed during training it will have encouraged the development of **laterals** – small side-shoots or branches. When the branches have been pinched out smaller branches or **sub-laterals** are produced. All this growth originates from the **axillary** buds, which are to be found where the leaves are attached to the stem – the **axils.** Leaves are arranged at regular intervals along a stem. The slight enlargement at the place where they grow from is called the **node** or **leaf joint.** Leaves are attached to the stem by small stalks which are known as **petioles.**

The flower is usually attached to the stem by a **pedicel** or flower stalk. Each flower is of similar structure, but some of the floral parts are not what they seem. The main coloured parts are referred to as the **tube, sepals** and **corolla.** It is these three which are commonly encountered in catalogues as 'T', 'S' and 'C', with the colour appended. The tube or **hypanthium** is the basal tubular part of the flower which extends and divides into the sepals – the part that most people believe are coloured petals. They form the **corolla** in which the protruding **anthers** and **stigma** are located. The anthers are the male element, the stigma the female, the former being borne on **filaments** and collectively known as the **stamens,** while the latter is supported by the **style.** The function of these floral parts is examined under Hybridisation (page 123). For the present, recognition is sufficient, for these are sometimes noted in descriptions of cultivars.

Fuchsia flowers are classified by gardeners and exhibitors into three categories – **single, semi-double** and **double.** Single flowers are those that have four petals. Semi-doubles have more than four petals but no

GLOSSARY

Bengal – dark purple-red colour.

Bract – modified leaves between the calyx and normal leaves.

Cast – infusion of another colour.

Cordate – heart-shaped.

Corolla – the petals as a whole.

Cultivar – a named plant of cultivated origin and maintained in cultivation. Not a plant of wild origin.

Damping off – a fungal disease. The stem rots and the plant collapses.

Elliptic – oval, but acute at each end.

Epiphytic – not depending upon soil for its sustenance. Often growing on other plants, but not parasitic.

Exserted – protruding.

Fluted – channelled or grooved.

Forma – a taxonomic division of a species often indicating variation in colour or in minor botanical detail.

Glabrous – smooth, devoid of hair.

Globose – round.

Hybrid – the result of the union of two distinct plants by cross-fertilisation.

Lanceolate – narrow, tapering at each end.

Lax – limp or pendulous mode of growth.

Leading growth – the main terminal shoot.

Madder – turkey-red.

Nectary – honey gland of a flower.

Ovate – egg-shaped.

Panicle – a branching flower stem.

more than eight and do not have a fully double appearance; this is often caused by the production of **petaloids** – petal-like structures which arise from sepals, stamens or other floral parts. Doubles are considered to be those flowers with more than the characteristic number of petals, an absence of petaloids, and a fully double appearance (some have more petals but do not look double). Abbreviations frequently used in catalogues and literature for these flower forms are : single 'SG'; semi-double 'SD': double 'D'.

Picotee edge – frilled edge

Raceme – an unbranched flower stem.

Recurved – bent moderately backwards into a curve.

Reflex(ed) – bent abruptly backwards.

Scandent – scrambling, creeping.

Self-branching – usually produces laterals freely without pinching out the terminal shoot.

Self-coloured – a single colour.

Short-jointed – leaf joints close together.

Spacer – device to hold branches apart at pre-determined distances.

Species – the wild form of a plant.

Species type – a term used loosely by gardeners to indicate a cultivar not far removed from a species and with most of its characteristics.

Species hybrid – a first generation hybrid between species which retains most of the parents characteristics. Not a wholly accurate botanical term, but one which is used by gardeners.

Sport – a mutation.

subsp. (subspecies) – a taxonomic division of a species. Sub-species are plants of lower rank and may only differ from the species in one or two small ways.

syn. – synonym.

Tyrian purple – crimson-purple.

var. (variety) – botanical varieties, not horticultural varieties which are more correctly cultivars. Of similar status to sub-species.

*Ideal as a spot plant with
its golden foliage, Genii
enjoys plenty of sun.
In Allan's opinion it should
be in every fuchsia grower's
garden. It is seen here
growing in the
Knaresborough Fuchsia and
Pelargonium Society's beds
at Harlow Car, Harrogate*

Further Reading

BOULLEMIER, Leo B. *The Checklist of Species, Hybrids and Cultivars of the Genus Fuchsia* (Blandford Press, 1985)

EWART, Ron *Fuchsia Lexicon* (Blandford Press, 1982)

GOULDING, E.J. *Fuchsias* (Bartholomew, 1973)

JENKINS, K. and MILLER, V.V. *Growing Fuchsias* (Croom Helm, 1979, 1983)

PROUDLEY, B. and V. *Fuchsias in Colour* (Blandford Press, 1981)

PUTTOCK, A.G. *Lovely Fuchsias* (John Gifford, 1959, 1971)

WILSON, S.J. *Fuchsias* (Faber and Faber, 1965)

WOOD, W.P. *A Fuchsia Survey* (Benn, 1950)

The authors and publishers would like to thank the following for their invaluable help in providing the photographs contained in this book:
John Glover: pages 7,15,22,23,30,35,39,59,74,122, 151,175,187,203,227,231.
Photos Horticultural (Michael and Lois Warren): pages 2,18,27,63,71,83,91,107,135,162,163,166, 179,206,211.
Enid Pyrah: pages 26,34,43,46,47,51,55,58,67,79, 87,95,103,106,110,118,126,127,131,139,143,146,150, 158,159,171,191,194,198,214,218,223,246,250.
All other photographs by Allan Waddington.

Acknowledgements

The many people I meet as I travel around the country lecturing, judging and exhibiting have all inspired me to write this book, but I owe a special debt of gratitude to my wife Joyce, who encouraged me to start writing and kept me motivated throughout.

I would like to thank Mrs Eileen Saunders for allowing me to use descriptions of fuchsia cultivars from the *Wagtails Fuchsia Books,* and for her help with the section on bonsai. Mrs Joan Goy was also a great help. Although she is secretary of the Wharfedale Fuchsia Society and the Harlow Fuchsia Group, she still found the time to type my original manuscript. Joan has been a constant source of help to me throughout our long association with the fuchsia.

Thank you also to the many nurserymen who have helped me with descriptions and samples of a wide range of varieties, and especially to Roy Sinton, who allowed me to visit his fuchsia nursery frequently and supplied me with many of his promising new cultivars to appraise. His Superstar is a must – and watch out for his Variegated Vivienne Thompson, to be released shortly.

David Downs, one of our top fuchsia showmen, was extremely kind in allowing me to photograph his prize-winning plants, and I must also thank Mrs Enid Pyrah for all her hard work in finding many more pictures for this book.

Finally, I would like to thank everyone in the fuchsia world who, over the past twenty years, has helped me in my quest for knowledge of these wonderful plants so that I, in turn, can pass my knowledge on through the pages of this book.

Allan Waddington

*A striking display of
fuchsias and other colourful
plants in baskets and pots
on a gable end wall.
This summer picture
provides a constant topic of
conversation
– and admiration –
for passing motorists*

251

Index

Page numbers in italics denote illustrations